Travelogue:
Greek everyday solutions to common problems

Curated by Loukas Angelou, Vasso Asfi, Costas Bissas

Travelogue: Greek everyday solutions to common problems is a book years in the making. Stemming from the project *DIY: Who's the designer?* by Papairlines, this publication serves as a visual journey of the spontaneous DIY culture throughout Greece and explores the connection between design as a practice and the artefacts by unknown individuals who create them.

DIY, or "Do It Yourself" is a term that seems to have sprung into mainstream culture when the best selling book by Samuel Smiles, *Self Help; with Illustrations of Character and Conduct*, was published in 1859. At first, its implementation was as a form of creative learning or productive leisure and then later, after WWII, as a way to affordably embellish the home. Today, DIY culture survives rebranded as the "makers movement" and makerspaces, where, using specialised shareable machinery, creators can produce increasingly sophisticated objects. As a way of thinking and thus creating our physical surroundings, one can presume that DIY is as old as the first human artefact. Could we not think of the first tool created by our prehistoric ancestors as a DIY object? Are the intricate machines created by Leonardo Da Vinci not the output of a similar mentality? And what about NASA's Perseverance rover on Mars?

One could claim that these objects were created for a specific reason: to cover specific human needs, utilising each era's available resources. Rather than being the output of mass production and widely available knowledge, these objects were the amalgamation of great insight, available resources and particular intent.

Seeing the world through the lens of DIY, one might try to identify its boundaries, with its ingenious combinations of available materials, used to fulfill immaterial needs. Understanding, exploring and pushing the inherent qualities and characteristics of a material, to forge new forms and functions, is closely related to human ingenuity and creativity; the kind exhibited by the anonymous creators in the following pages, as well as established creators (individuals, companies or brands). The latter are responsible for guaranteeing a well-studied, eco- and socio-friendly design, making best use of available resources, and deeply understanding human problems and needs. Anonymous creators might not bear the same responsibility but, by leading through example, they help us generate new thoughts, shed light on unexpected needs with more or less humour, technical competence and accidental aesthetics. They remain doers and creators, planning or arranging elements to accomplish a particular purpose which, according to the renowned industrial designer Charles

Eames in an interview with curator Mme. L'Amic of the Musee des Arts Decoratifs, is the definition of design. In that sense they are inadvertently designers, in fact they are "DIY designers".

Papairlines are a team of designers, Loukas Angelou, Vasso Asfi and Costas Bissas. With an applied interest in how ideas are born, they began photographing objects by unknown creators before 2012, mainly to satisfy their own curiosity as to how non-designers act creatively, composing solutions to problems and needs while filling in design omissions uncatered for by the existing infrastructure and equipment. As the team's thoughts on *DIY: Who's the designer?* matured and their personal photographic collection grew, conversations around every new found photo provoked a desire to involve more contributors in the project. New perspectives could bring invaluable fresh information and interesting objects from distant and remote locations. To the question "What ingenious objects might exist in Greece that have been created by DIY designers?", the team responded with an open call to professional and amateur photographers asking for images from all over the country.

In the following pages, the reader can find contributions from different parts of Greece, by photographers who are not necessarily the object creators, but successfully capture the essence of these artefacts. Objects that find their place in the home, the garden, by the sea, in public spaces and which discuss mobility, aesthetics and the built environment, created by people who wear their creative hat to obtain the spontaneous role of housekeeper, botanist, castaway, mayor, driver, curator, tailor or builder. And while each creator's motivation is mostly unknown, the photos manage to generate optimism and the satisfaction that inventiveness has no end. People will continue to intervene in their surroundings and, as civilization and technical abilities evolve, future DIY objects will cover new needs with novel and ingenious combinations of raw materials.

After all, though it might not always be important to know who the designer is, it is vital that creators never stop creating, that they are always willing to take up new roles, and that they never take themselves too seriously!

Loukas Angelou, Vasso Asfi, Costas Bissas
Papairlines

I can only imagine what it was like to stroll down a street and observe the work of the *builder*, to visit a friend who turns out to be a *curator*, or to take a walk in the countryside and get acquainted with the *tailor*.

What a documented wealth! It's almost like following a very observant human-camera entity, that has been making new friends. All the new friends are designers. Apart from the builder, the curator and the tailor, there's also the housekeeper, the botanist, the driver, the castaway and the mayor.

The observations that this human-camera entity has been making are active and poignant, and they speak to a designer role under constant negotiation. Sometimes we've gotten to know designers as the ones who make (with so-called virgin material) and who perhaps make for mass production – or at least for a consumer.

What I find interestingly characteristic of all these DIY designers is that they break away from many of these designer traits. The builder, curator, housekeeper, botanist, driver, tailor, castaway and mayor do not try to make something new for the market. Rather the opposite: they are making something out of what is already at hand – and the process of making is directed by very specific situations. It's neither for the market nor made for the masses. It is unique and crafted with the materials at hand, so in that sense the designer's role overlaps with that of the crafter.

The documentation in this book makes it obvious that there is a need for these DIY designers in a plethora of places: urban, rural, private, public, on land and at sea. The breadth of locations tells us about the importance of the work that the DIY designers have been conducting – what would have happened otherwise in these situations? The pictures convince me that the work that has been created is keeping up with everyday life for basic survival: governance (the mayor), beauty (the curator), mobility (the driver), oikos as in shelter and nutrients (the botanist, the housekeeper, the builder and the tailor).

Interestingly, there are no humans in the pictures. Who are they really – the makers and the users? Are they hiding because they are medicalised as hoarders? I mean, the throw-away culture and disposability that has been built into so much of modern western life doesn't really support the kind of storing that I suggest some of these DIY designers have been practising and benefitting from.

Maybe, if there were more of us that accumulated bits and pieces that might one day be of use, combined with fewer new products, then this practice might actually make a difference to earthly survival. If we recognised that we live in a broken world, then the DIY designers would be the cure, rather than the disease: extractivating from what already exists above ground and not demanding the mining of new resources.

What if we try to think of fixing the broken world from another perspective: is hoarding causing the crisis? Do the stored materials need to be circulated all the time, rather than stored in someone's private storage space? Is this where we start to think of yet another new designer role where there is a hotline that people in need can call and have things fixed and pimped up? What else do the DIY designers have in their storage?

To move out of the DIY into something more like Do It Together, we can ask ourselves whether these private storage spaces can be opened up for others to come and forage. What impact can these healing DIY designers achieve in a broken world? Could these designs be repeated somewhere else, by somebody else, in order to make a difference beyond the specific location that the human-camera entity has captured so eloquently? If we take design to be a practice of turning the future into a preferred one, we must also be able to imagine what that preferred future could be like.

Looking for the preferred future opens the question of where imagination comes from.

I take the observations (that this camera-human entity brings to us) as a source of inspiration and as a source of imagining a future that works for the survival of the earth, humans, other living entities and things by connecting and healing what has been broken.

Åsa Ståhl
Senior Lecturer in Design
Linnaeus University, Sweden

Access ladder
Aluminium ladder, rope

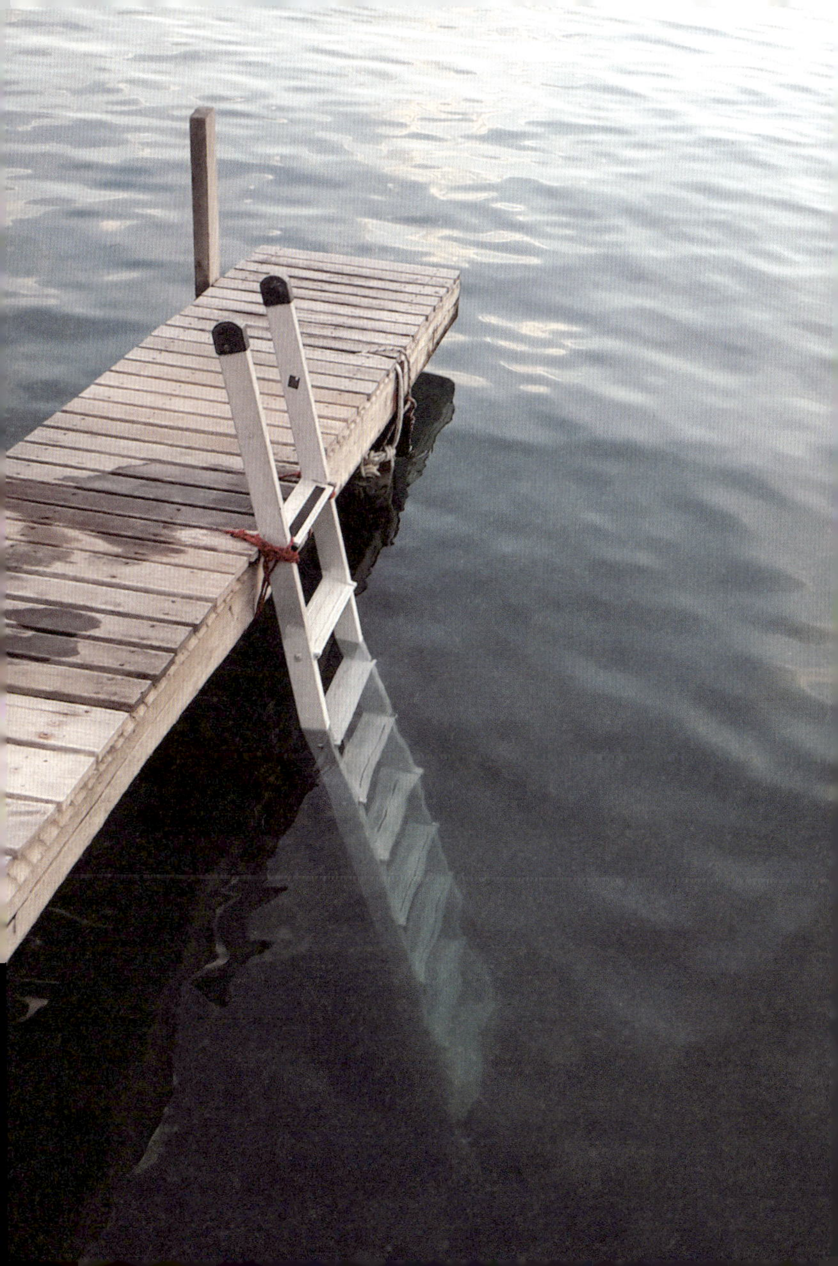

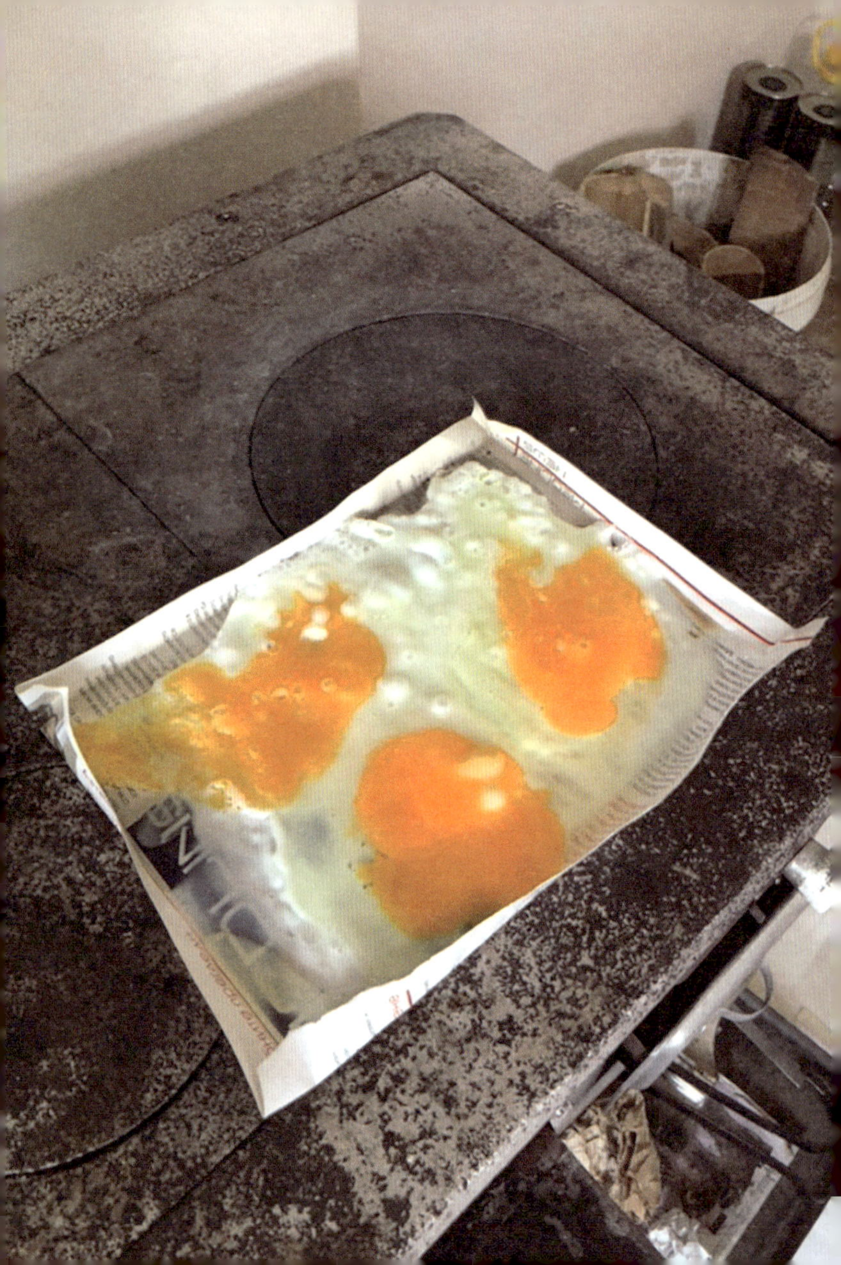

Frying pan
Folded newspaper

Location unknown
Nadia Todorova

Planter
VW Beetle bonnet, chain, wire

Koropi
Yorgos Fakinos

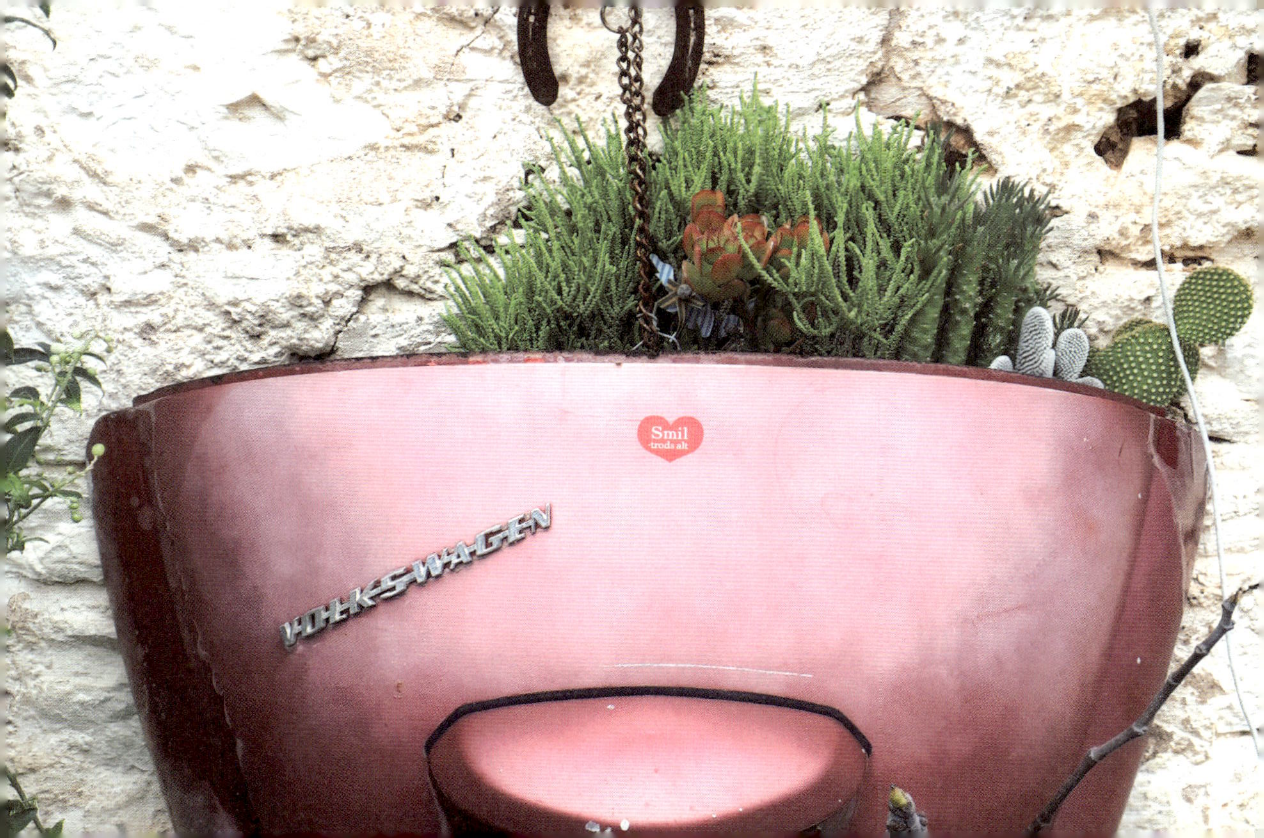
Smil
-trods alt
VOLKSWAGEN

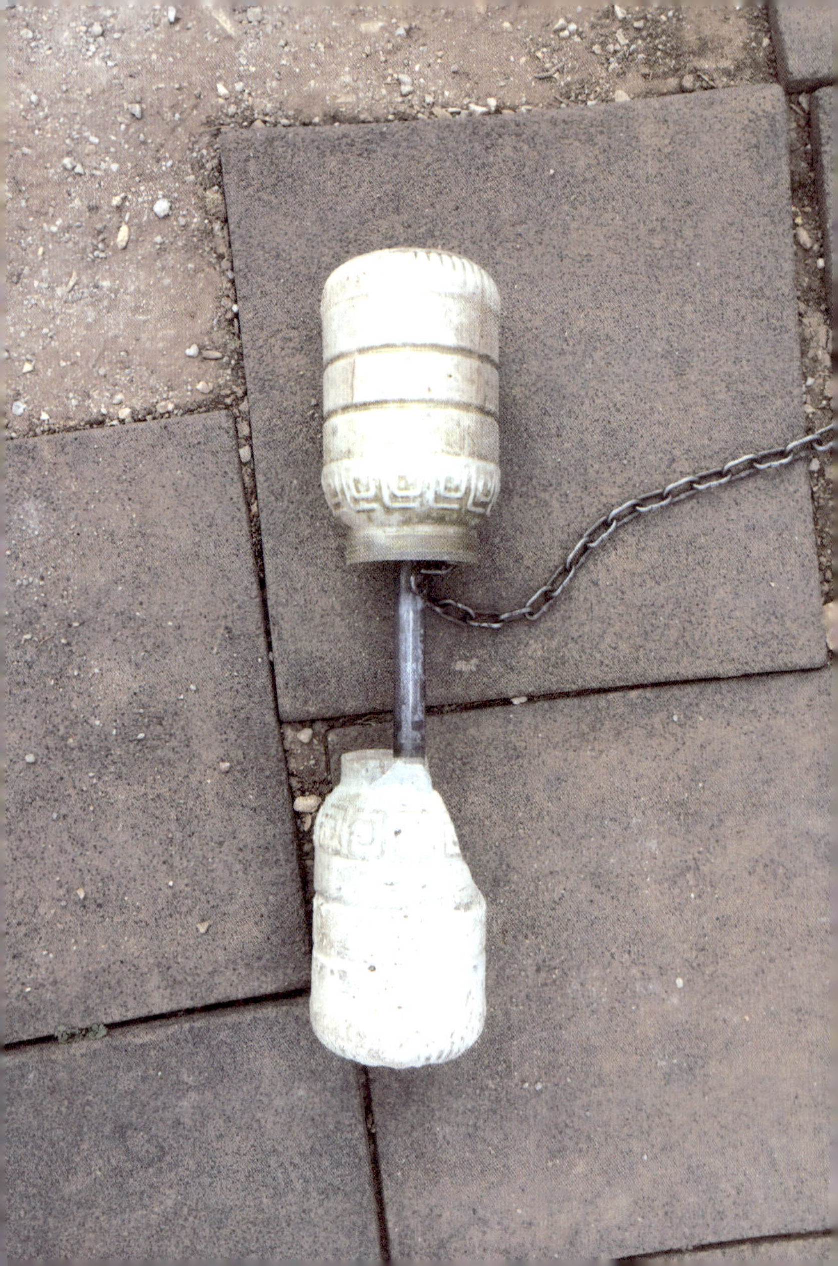

Dumbbell

Concrete, chain, metal pipe, food container

In recent years, municipalities have been installing outdoor gym equipment to help citizens stay fit. Following this trend, a group of residents have created their own outdoor urban DIY fitness area. Here, this designer has offered the public a dumbbell, while making sure it is securely chained to the workout area and cannot go missing.

Athens
Papairlines

Protective fence
Rope, interior doors

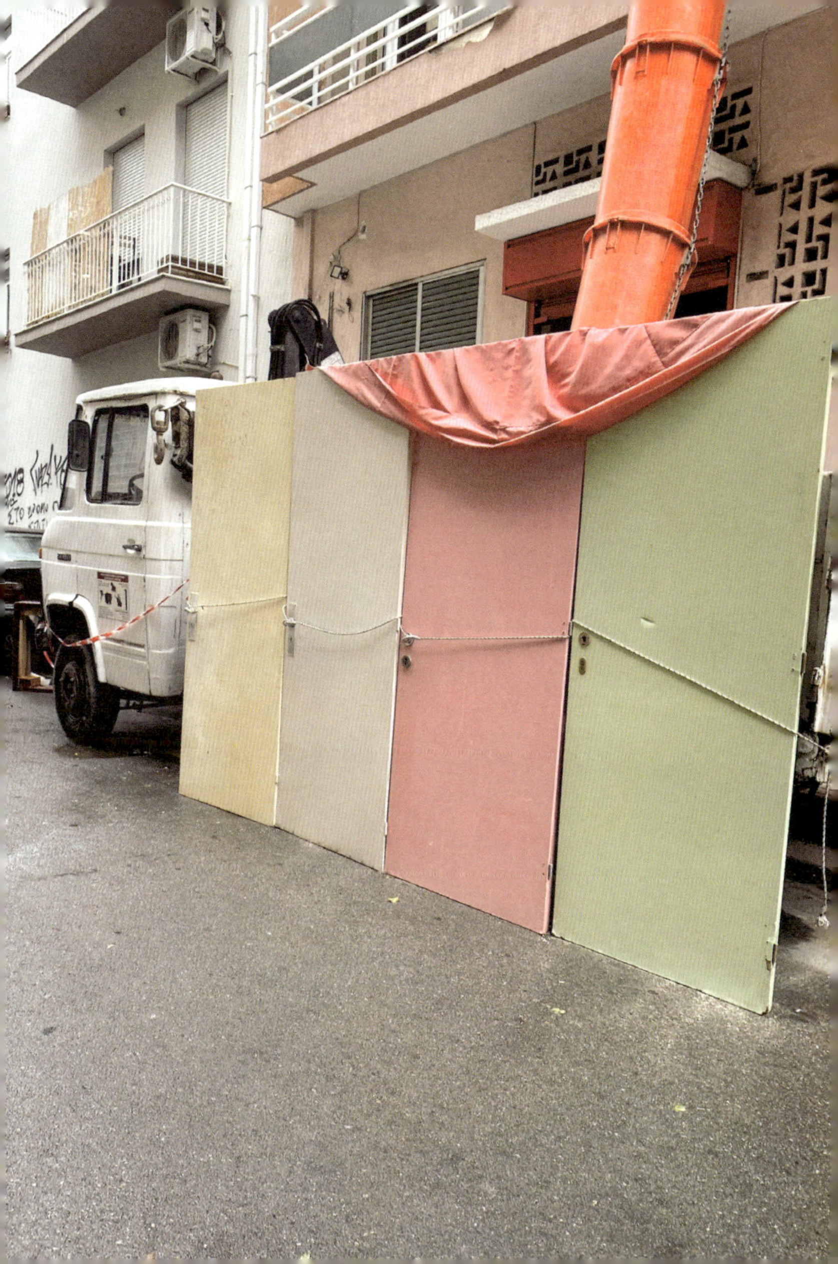

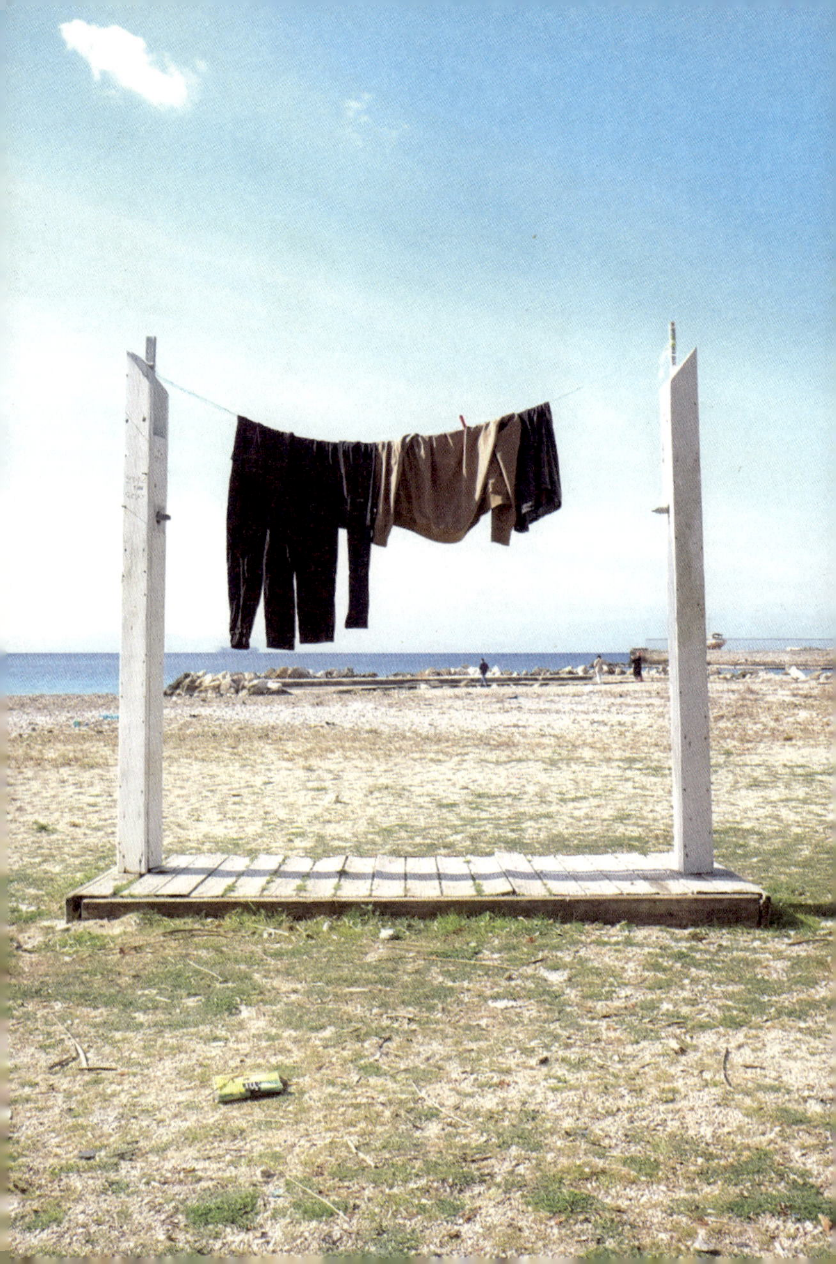

Drying rack
Rope, existing shower platform

Athens
Giorgos Georgakopoulos

Personal temple
Christmas ornaments, various contruction materials, acrylic rope

Katakolo
Giorgos Georgakopoulos

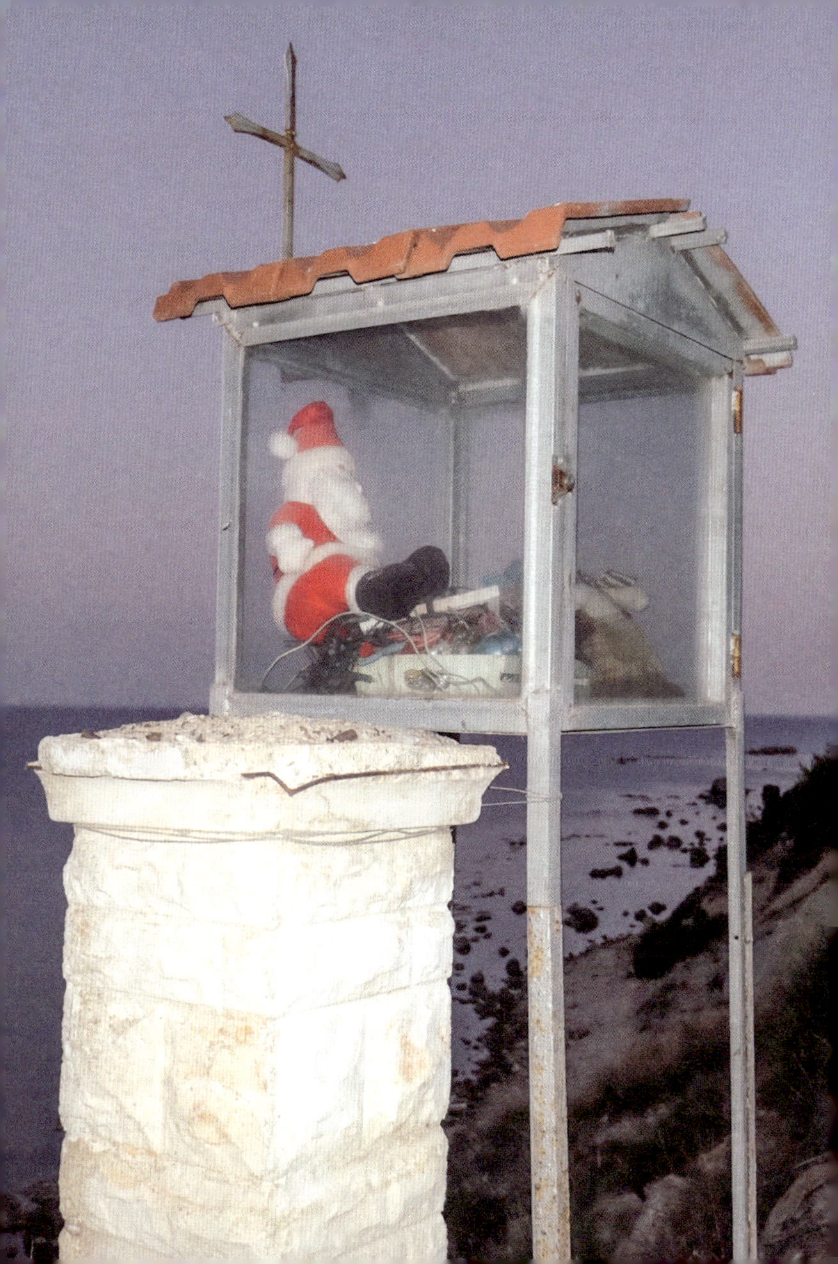

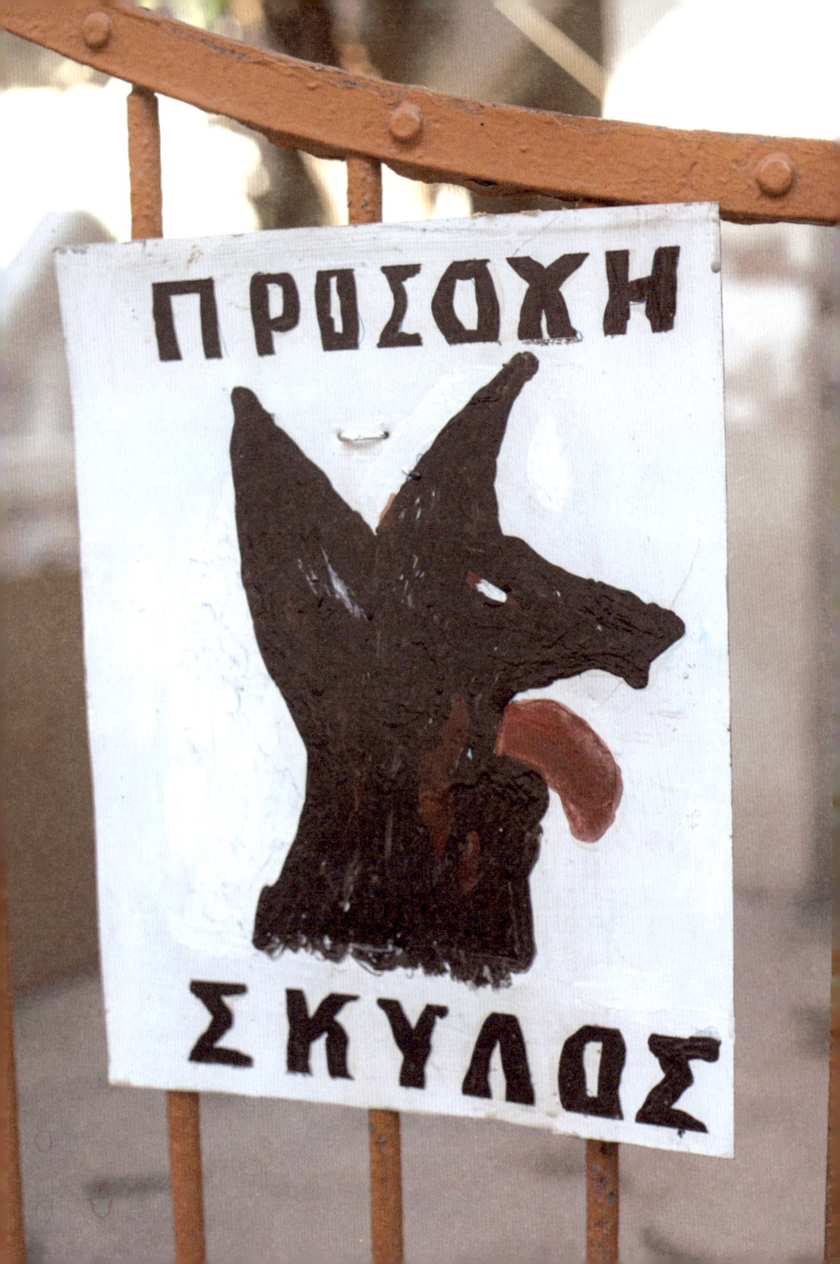

ΠΡΟΣΟΧΗ

ΣΚΥΛΟΣ

Warning sign
Metal sheet, paint, metal wire

Chios
Manos Chatzikonstantis

Boat base

Barrel, breakwater, stone

Mesolongi

Sotiris Patronis

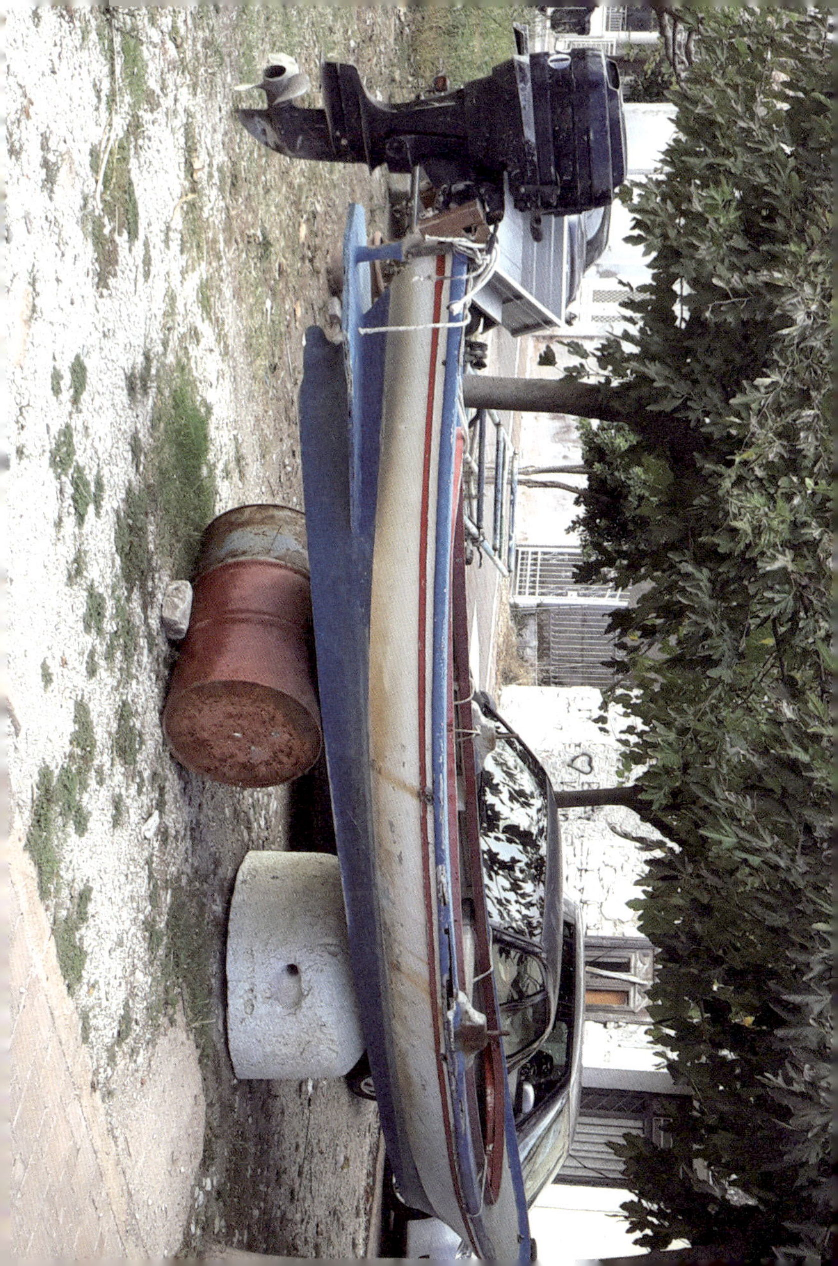

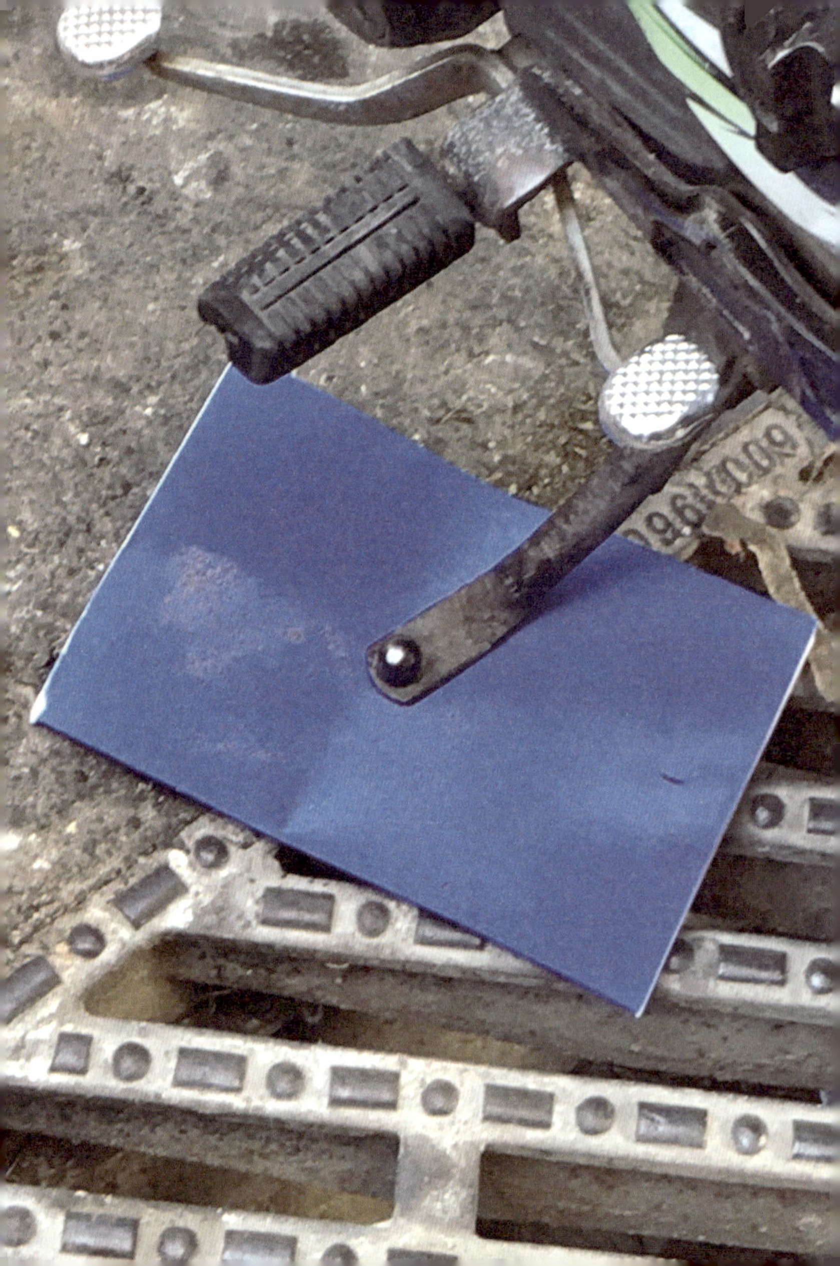

Motorcycle stand stabiliser
School notebook

Athens
Stathis Mitropoulos

Table lamp
Perforated aluminium pot, metal net, hookah, cable, metal base

Samos
Konstantina Mitataki

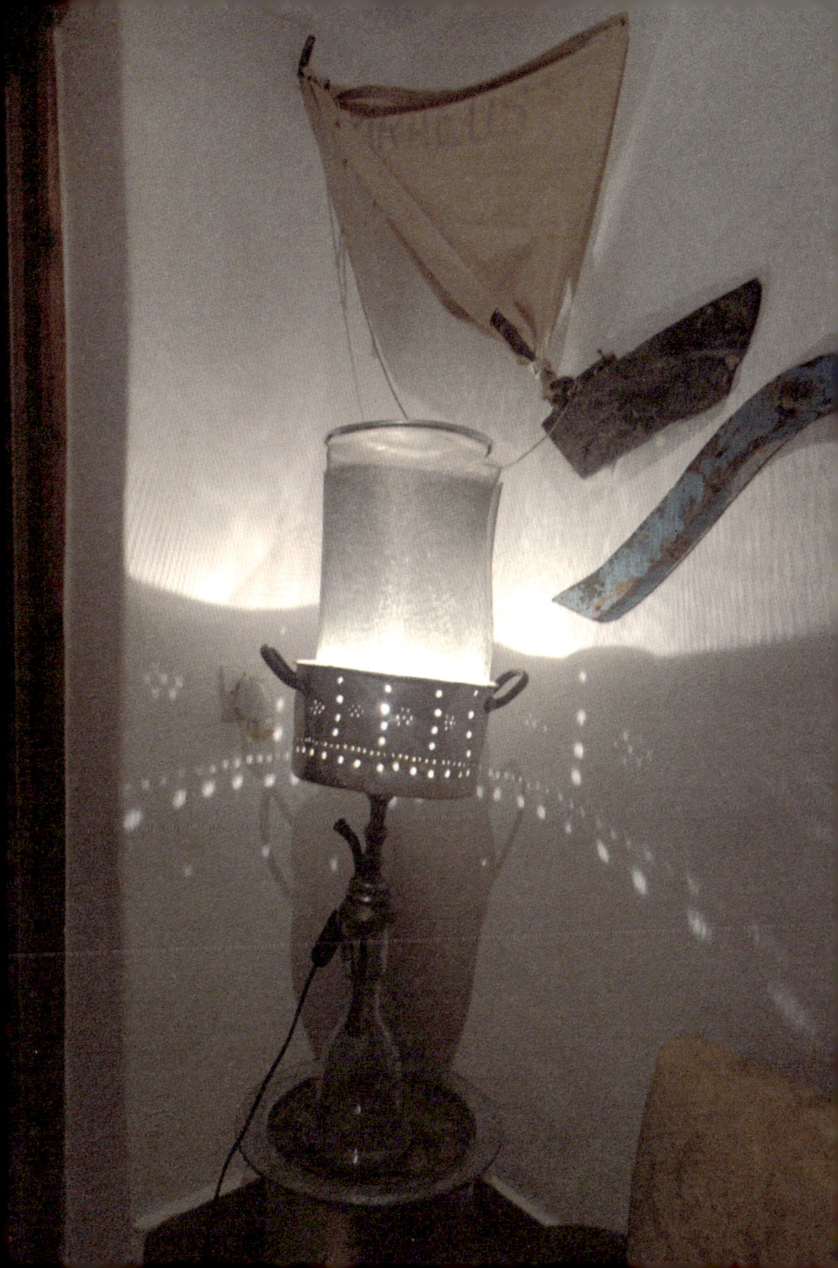

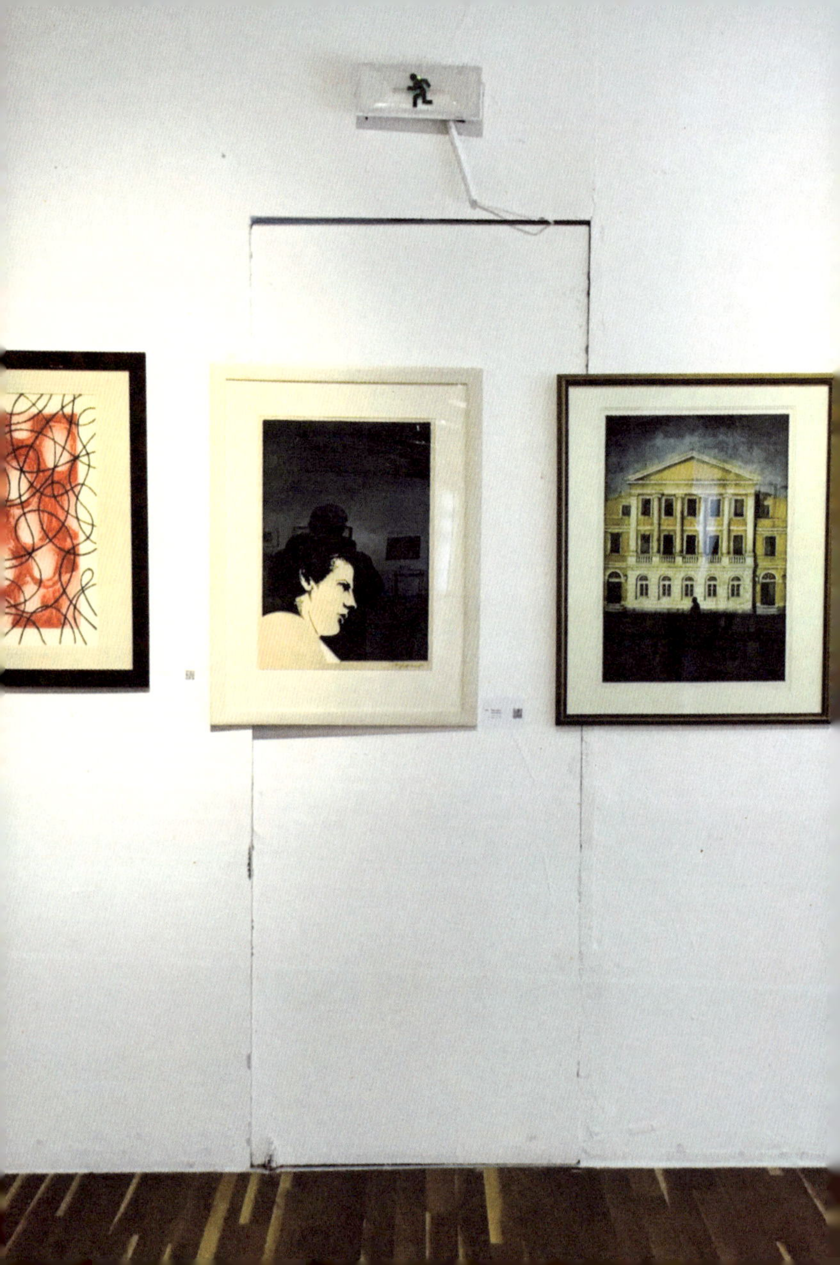

Curatorial camouflage

Framed artworks, nails, door, fire exit,

Athens

Stathis Mitropoulos

Anchors
Plastic basket, concrete, steel bars

Many Greeks live near the sea and some own small boats. But marinas and safe docks may not be available everywhere. So, if the state does not provide a proper marina, individuals may submerge their own DIY objects to tie their boats safely close to the coast.

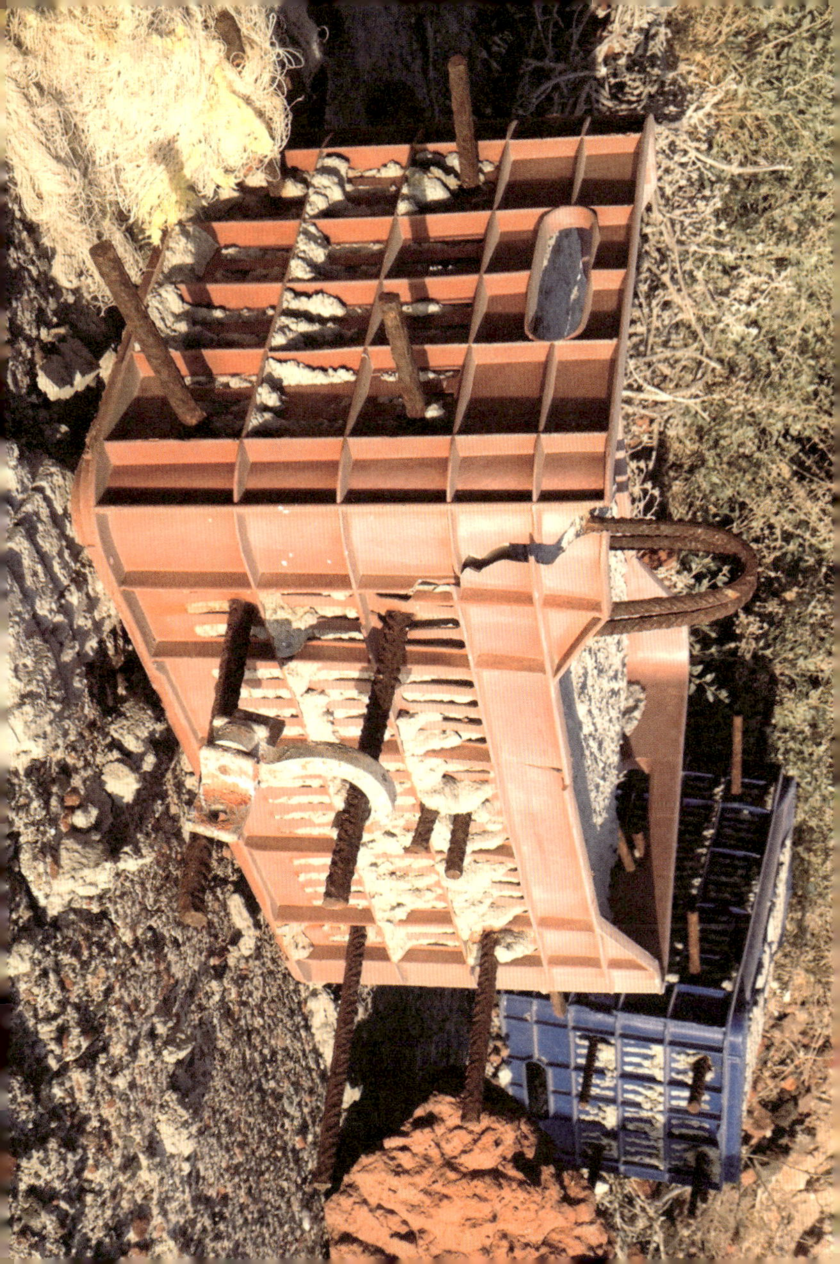

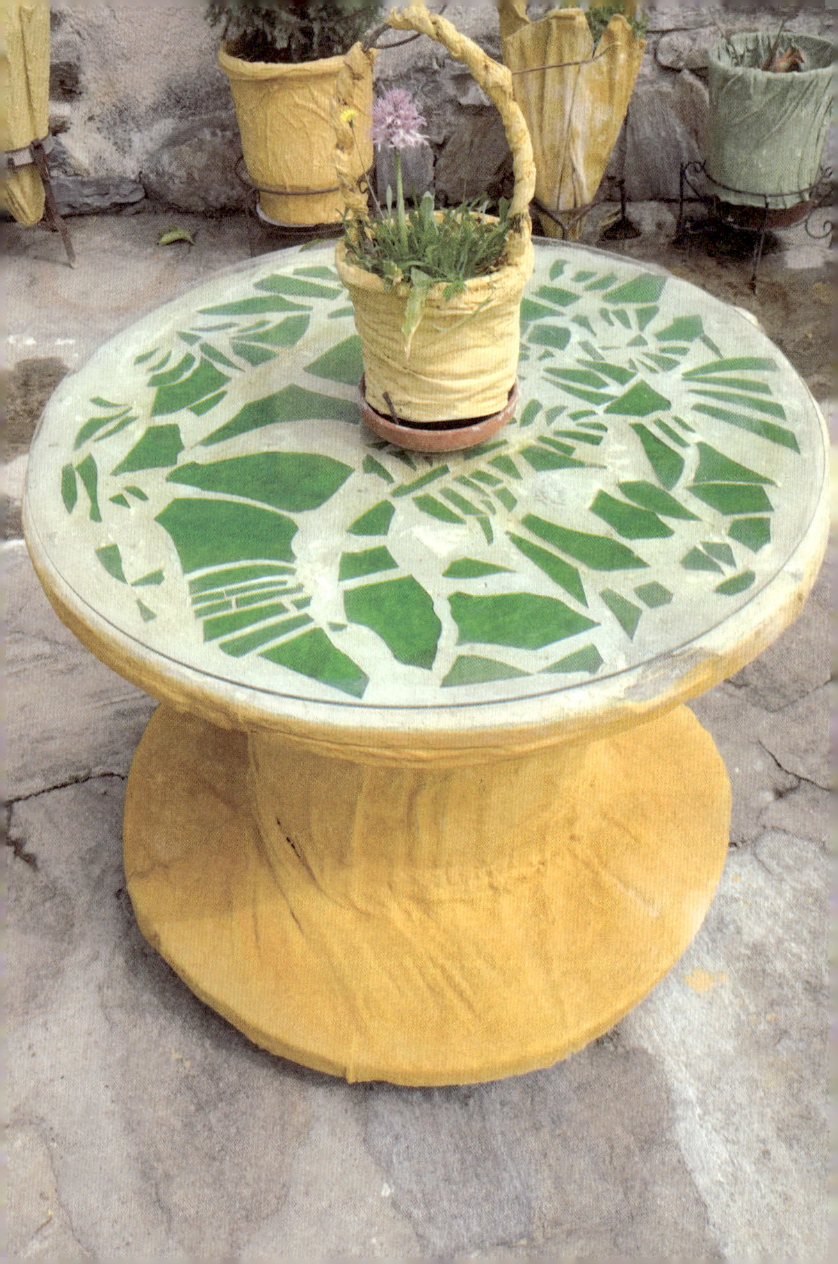

Table
Cable reel, cement soaked towels, broken ceramic tiles, glass

Abandoned wooden cable reels are a common sight in remote areas around Greece. Discarded after their original use, they get picked up to be re-used as tables in residential settings. Here, the designer made a version that is fully customised with the use of fabric, glue and colours.

Samos
Konstantina Mitataki

Motorbike wind-proofing
Tape, cardboard, tie-wraps

Athens
Ioannis Sclavos

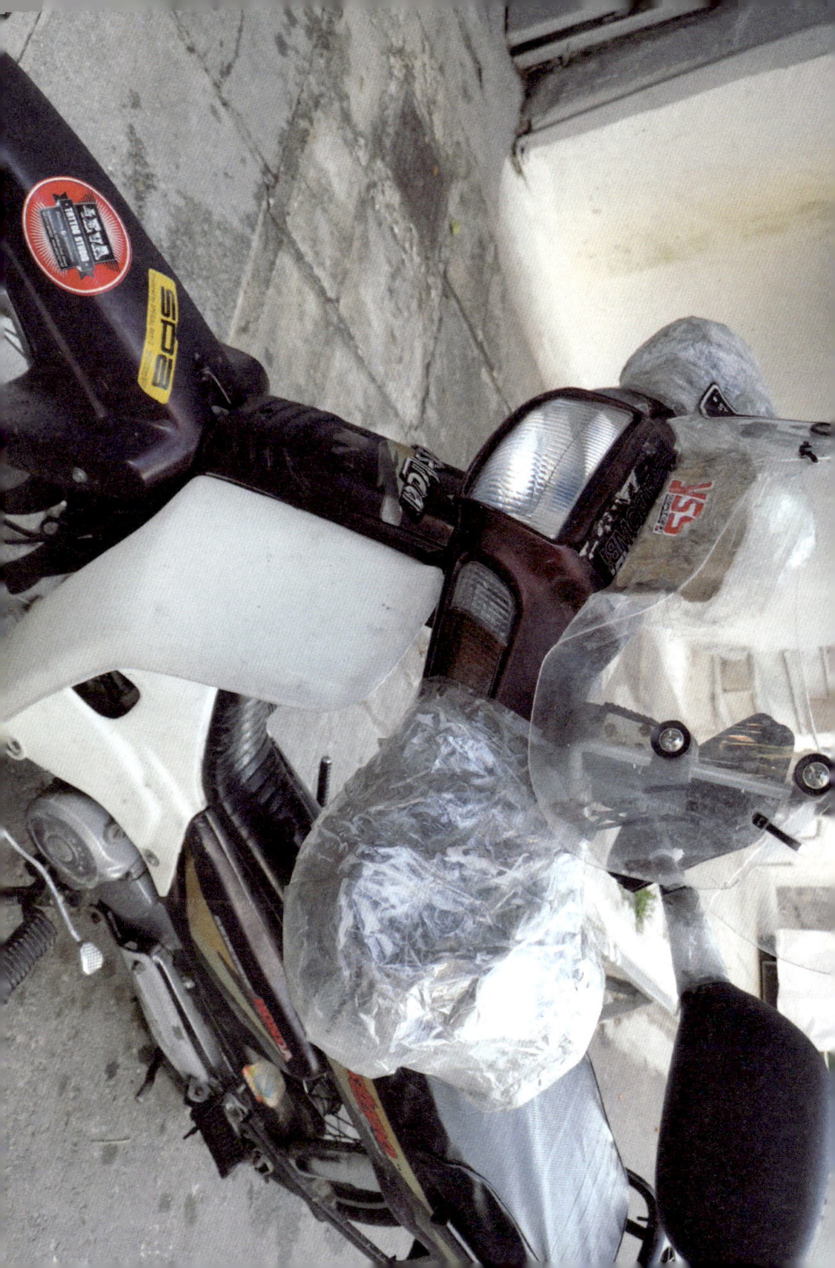

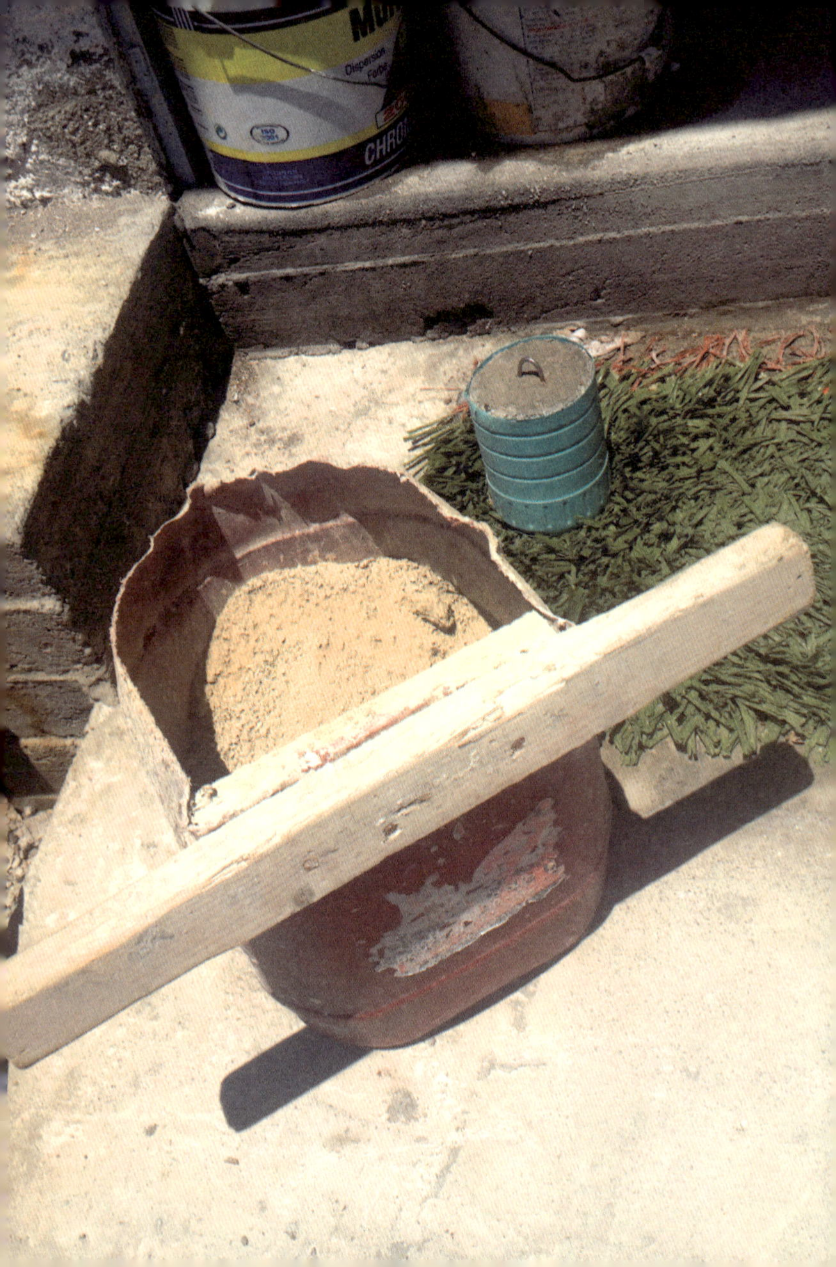
Dispersion

Construction material carryall

Plastic container, wood, nails

The 60s were a time of great construction in Greece. This DIY object is considered iconic, as it has been used to carry sand and cement on builders' backs. Some say that if Greek concrete buildings are what they are today, they owe it to this object.

Observation canopy, throne
Wood, stones, tarpaulin, armchair

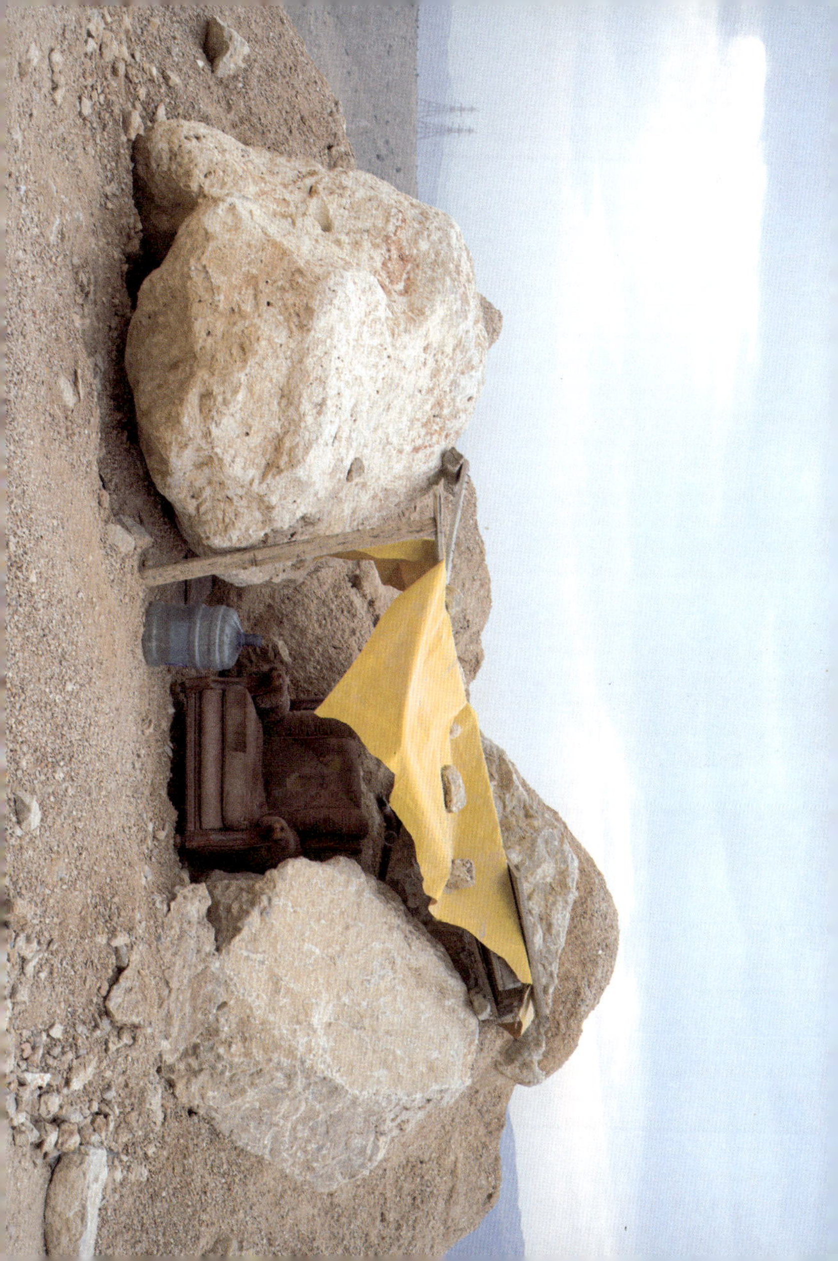

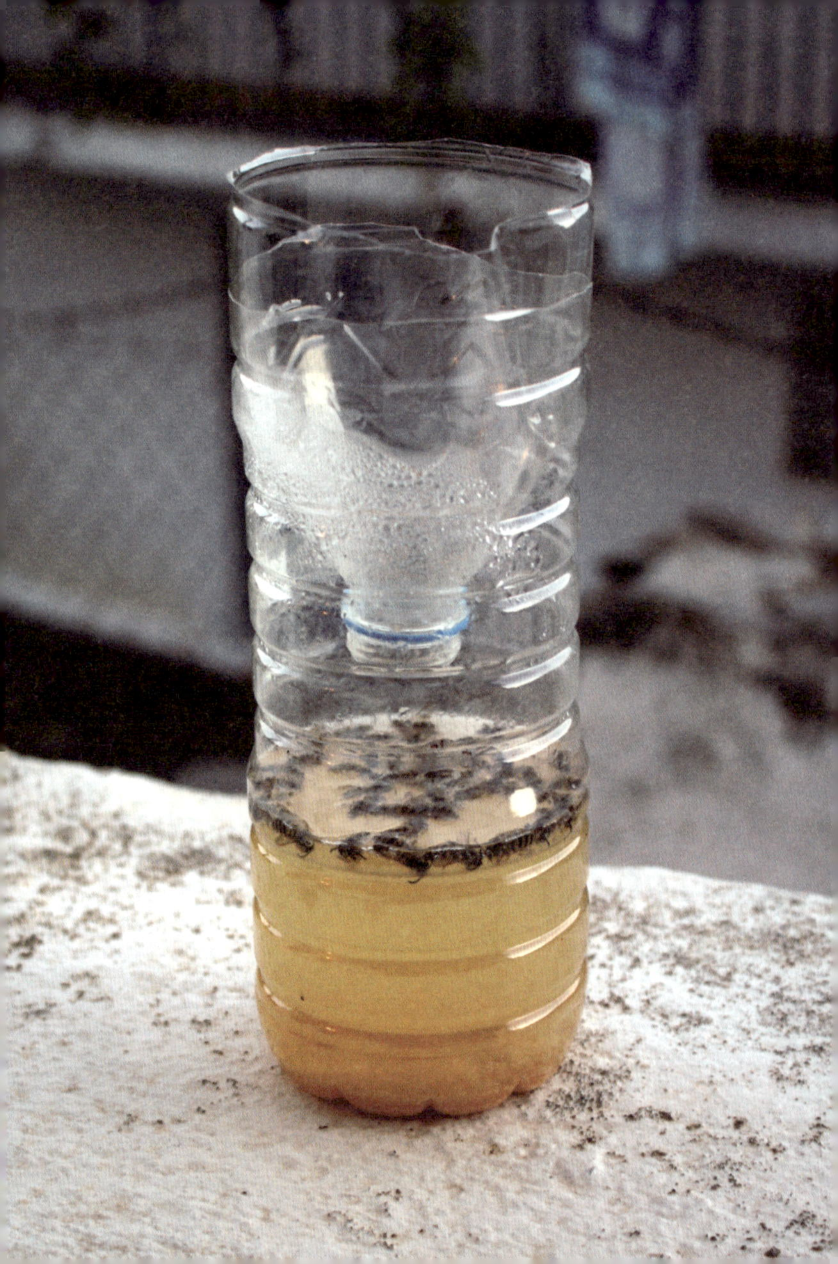

Wasp trap

Plastic bottle, water, orange juice

Meganisi
Papairlines

Basketball backboard
Reclaimed plywood, basketball hoop with net

Mesolongi
Manos Chatzikonstantis

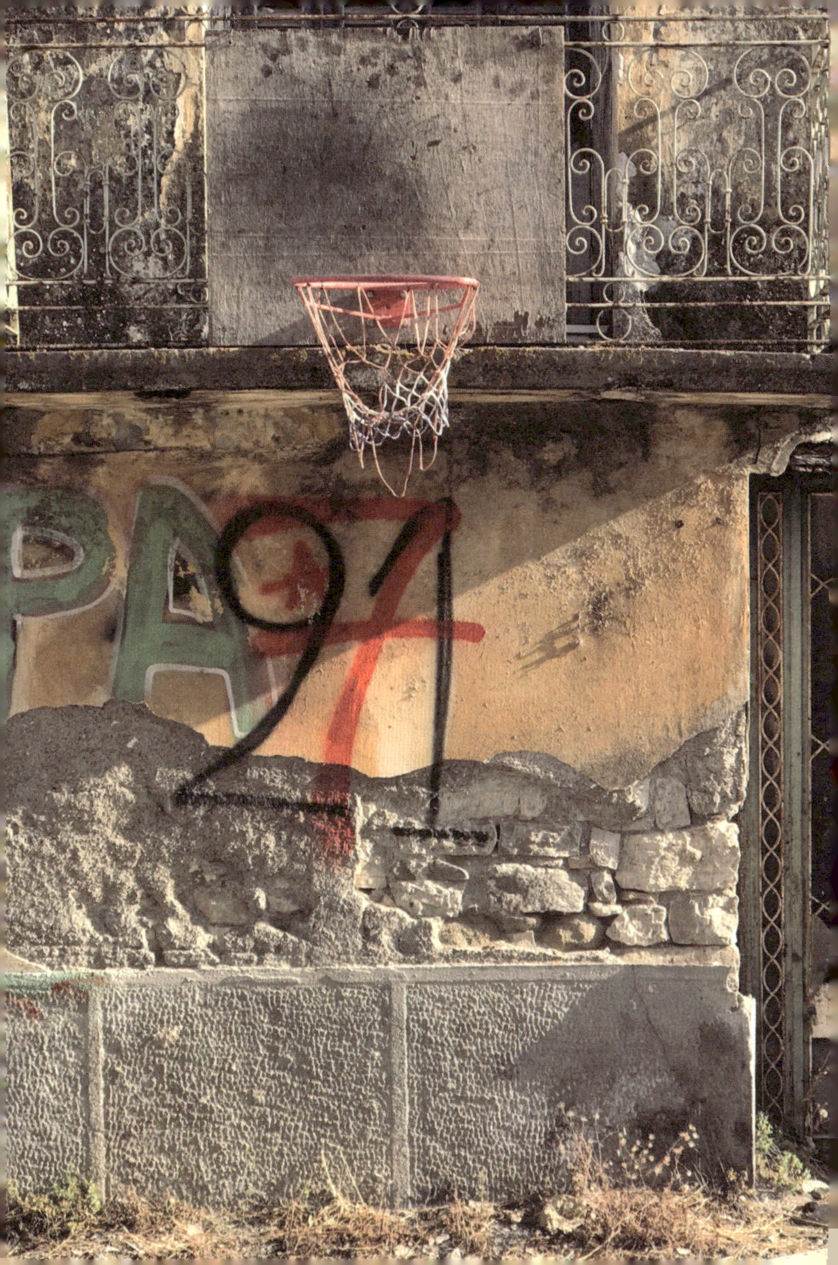

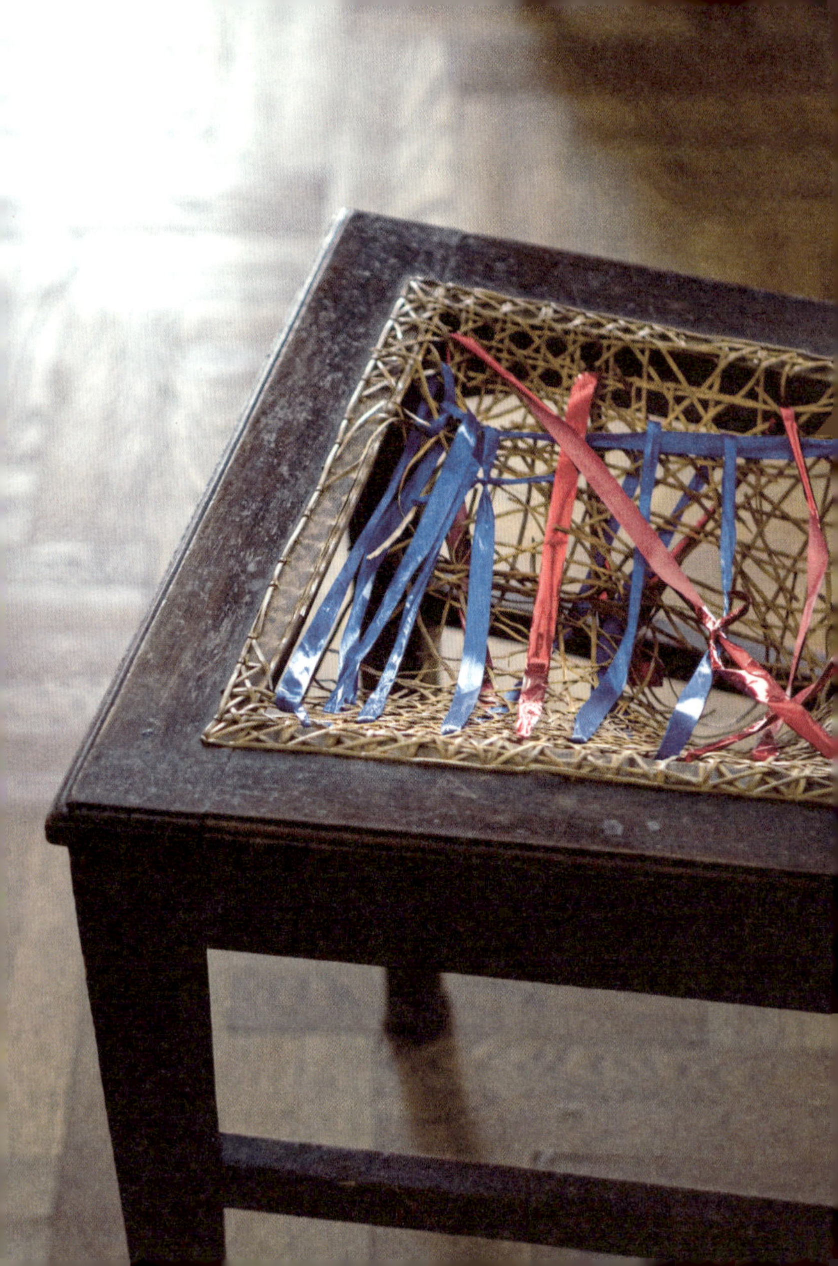

Wicker seat repair
Gift wrapping ribbons in metallic finish

Athens
Manos Chatzikonstantis

Planter

Wellies, paint

Samos

Konstantina Mitataki

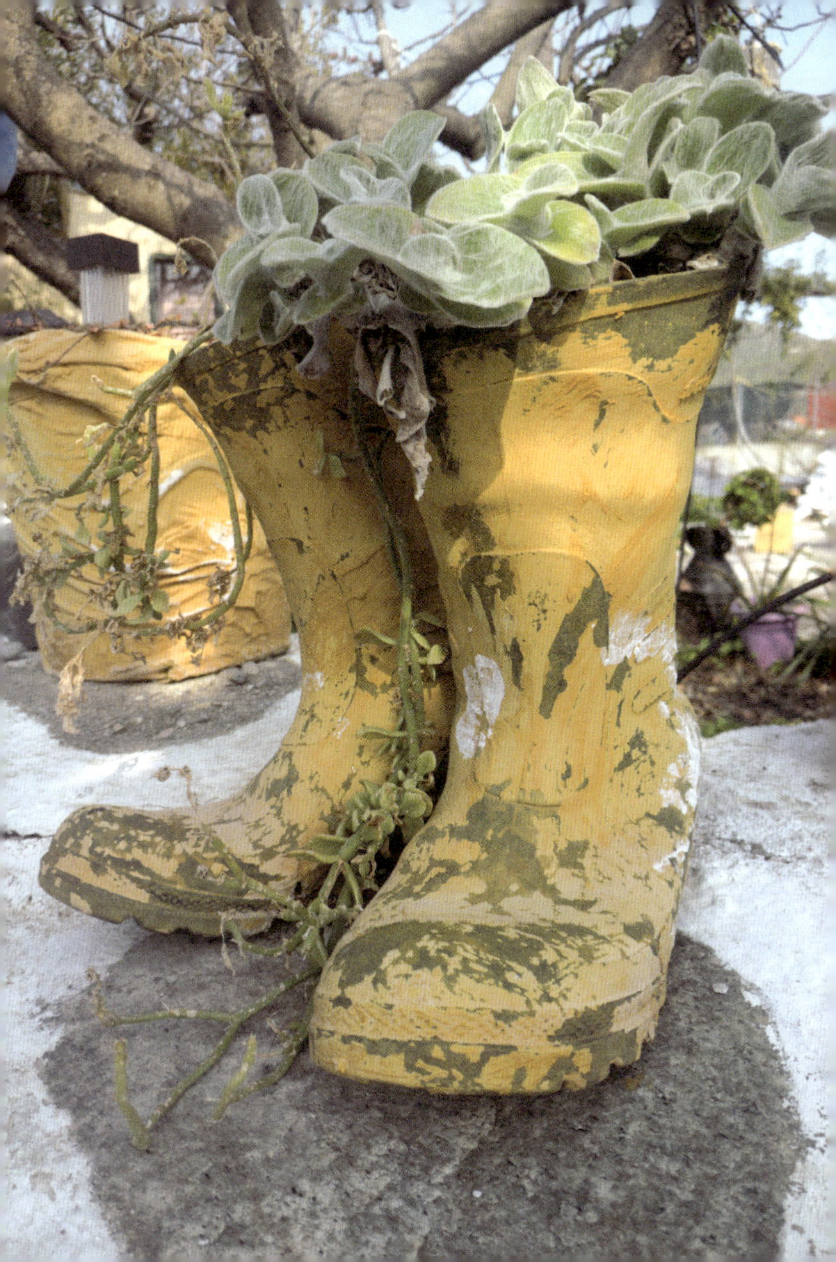

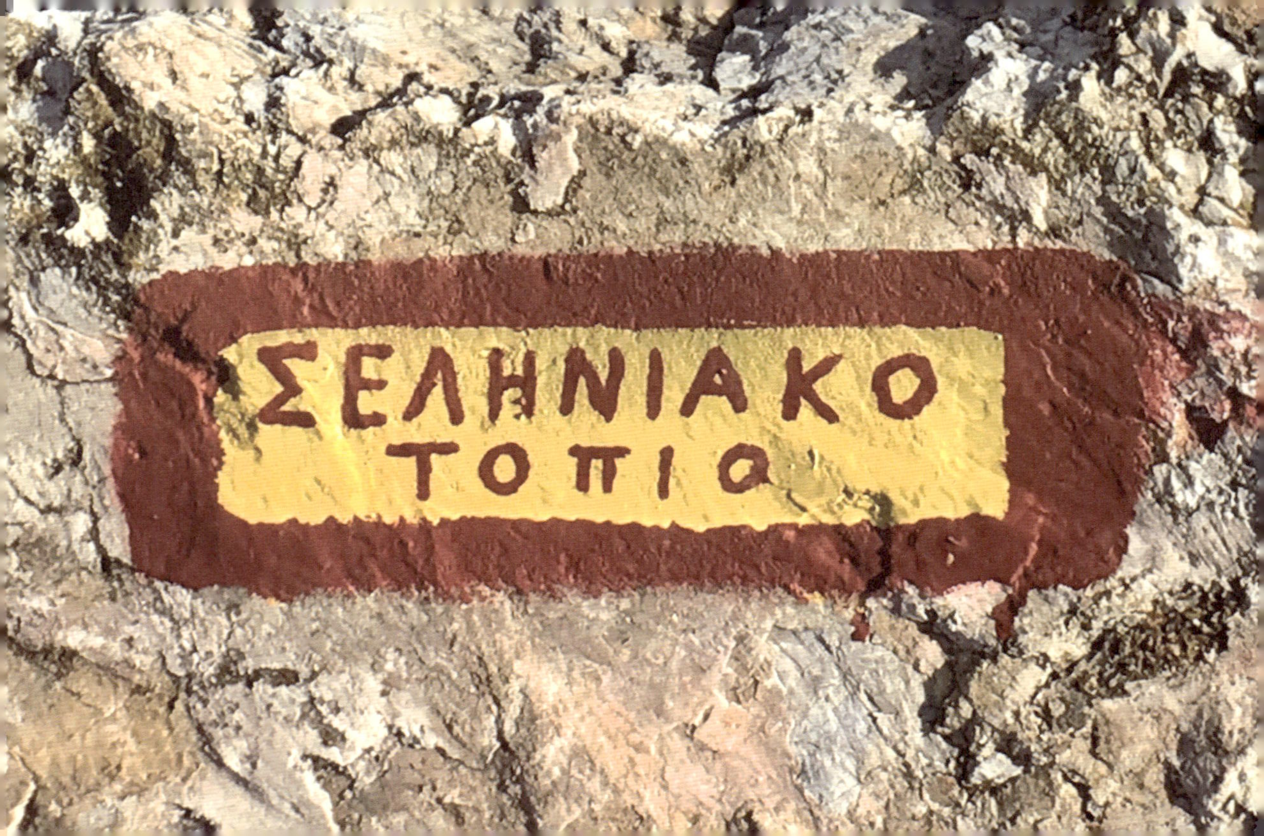
ΣΕΛΗΝΙΑΚΟ
ΤΟΠΙΟ

There are times when the built environment is so desecrated and abused that it looks like the surface of the moon. Having an apt ability to discern this, this DIY designer created a fictional location sign that reads “Moonscape” in Greek, which leads to a change of perspective.

Athens
Stathis Mitropoulos

<u>Water flow gutter</u>
Plastic tube cut in half

Turning on the faucet of a public fountain can be a splashy process, especially if the handle is located in the center of the water basin. This DIY designer has made sure that water hits the ground at a smooth angle so everybody leaves the site unsplashed.

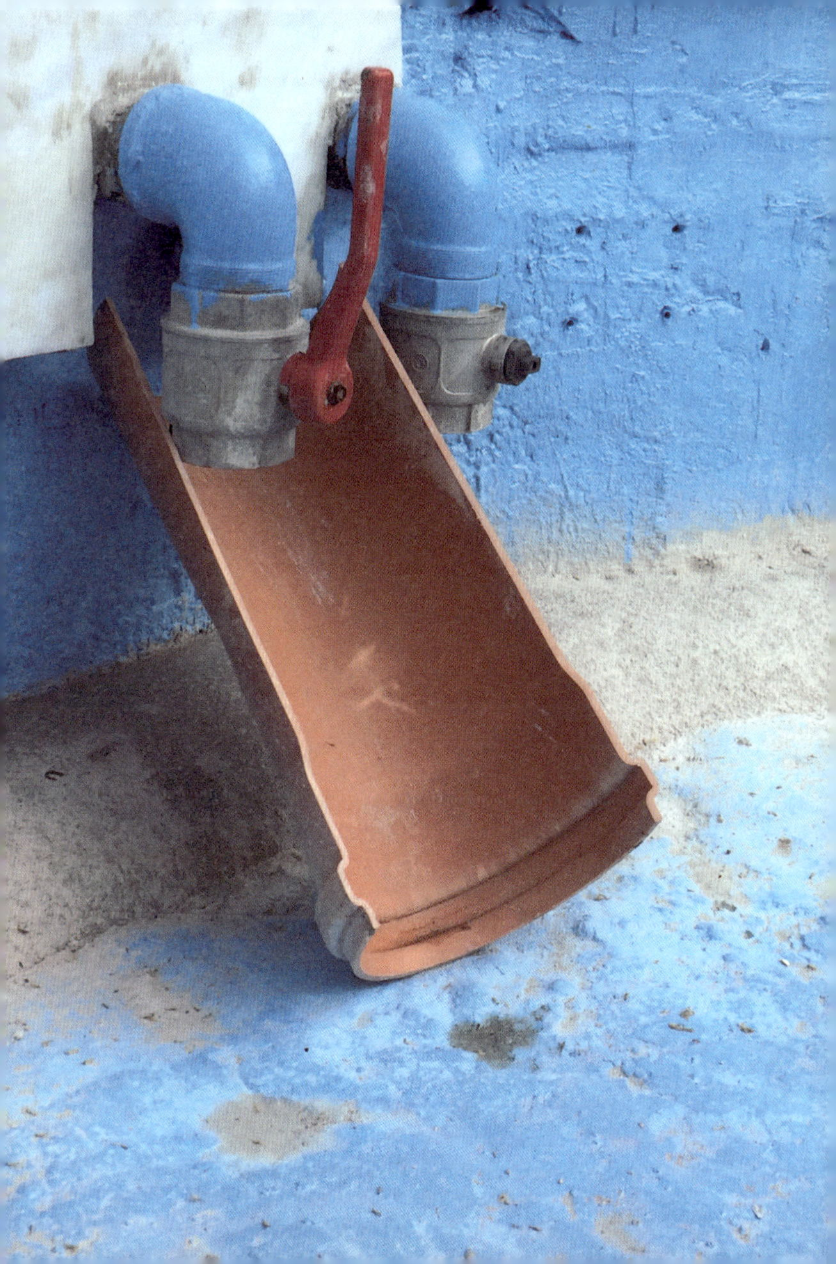

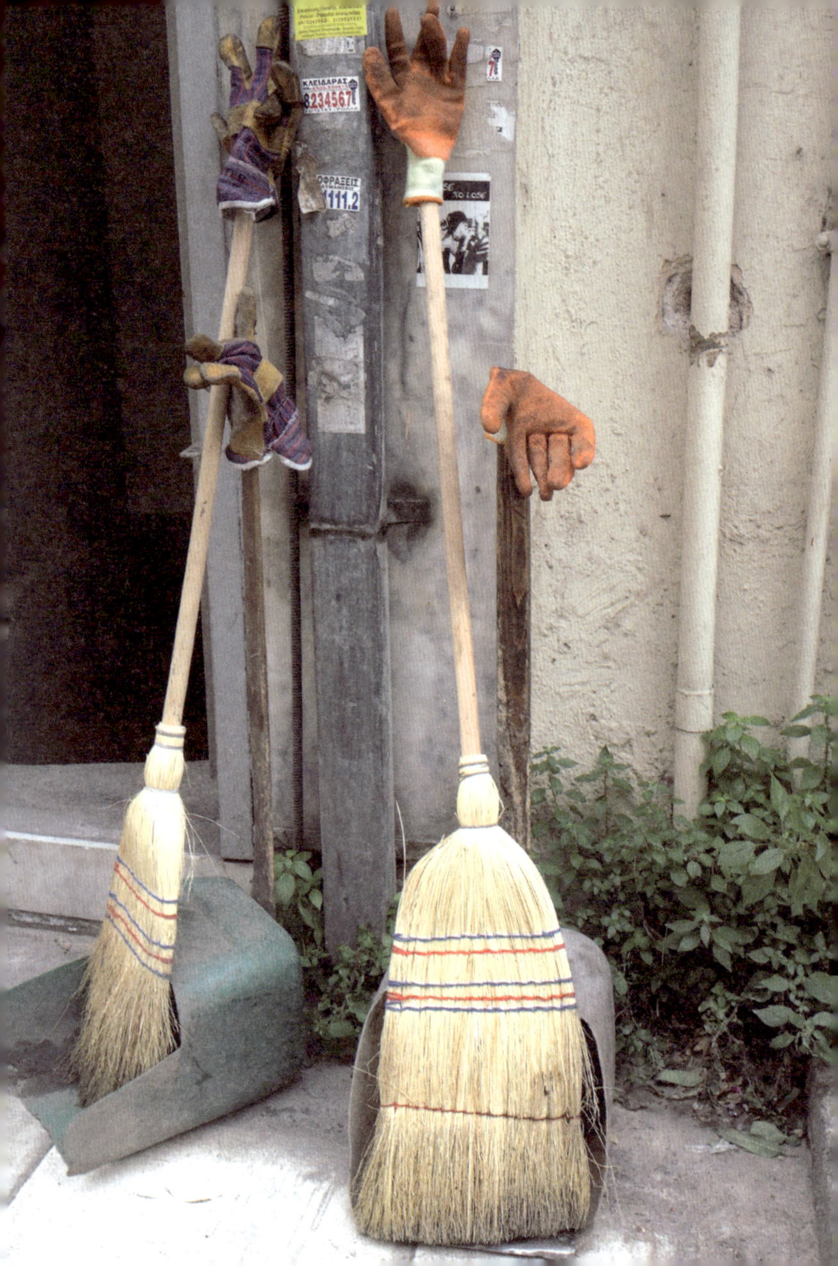
ΚΛΕΙΔΑΡΑΣ
8234567

Heavy-duty dustpan

Plastic container, broom stick, gloves

Tapestry boat cover
Kilims, threads

Corfu
Manos Chatzikonstantis

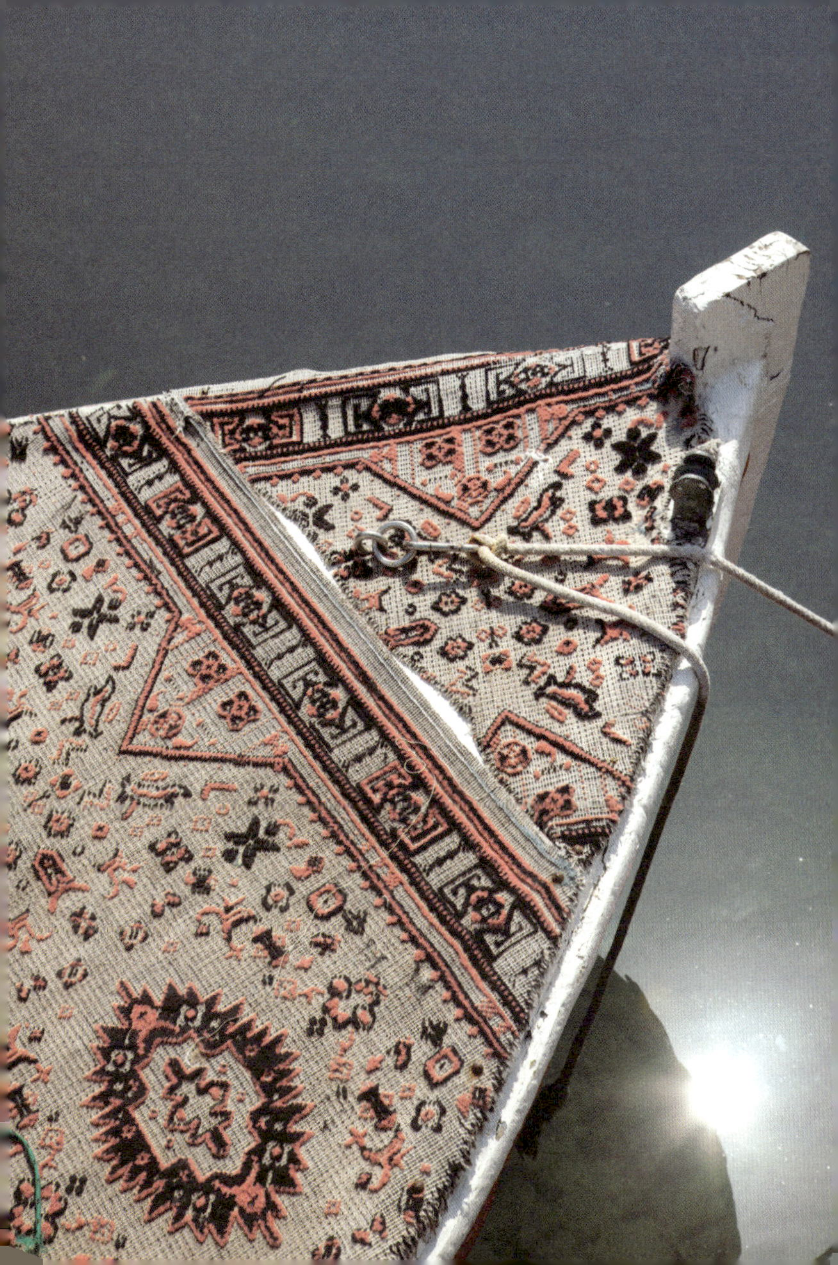

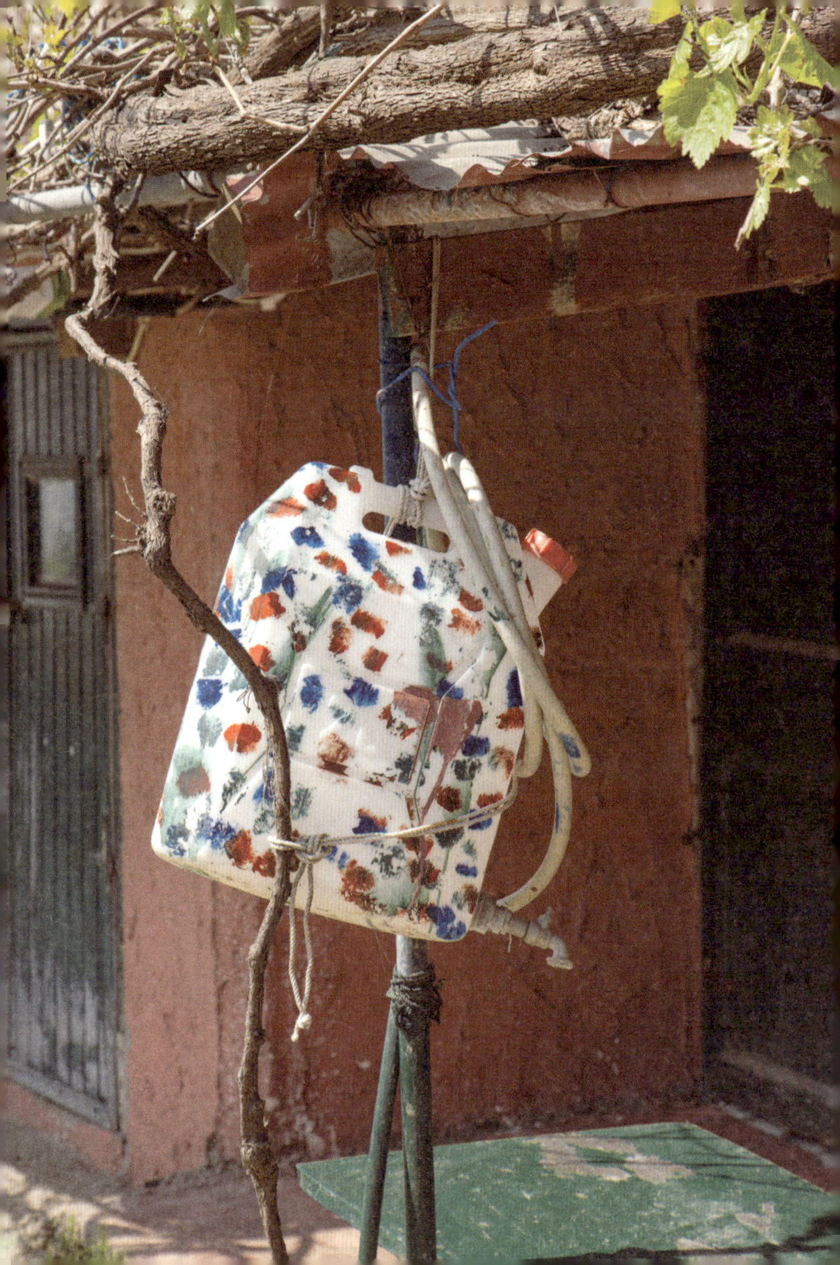

Outdoor faucet

Plastic container, faucet, rope, cable, watering hose

Corfu

Manos Chatzikonstantis

Wall-mounted knife storage
Broken loundspeaker, screws

Samos
Konstantina Mitataki

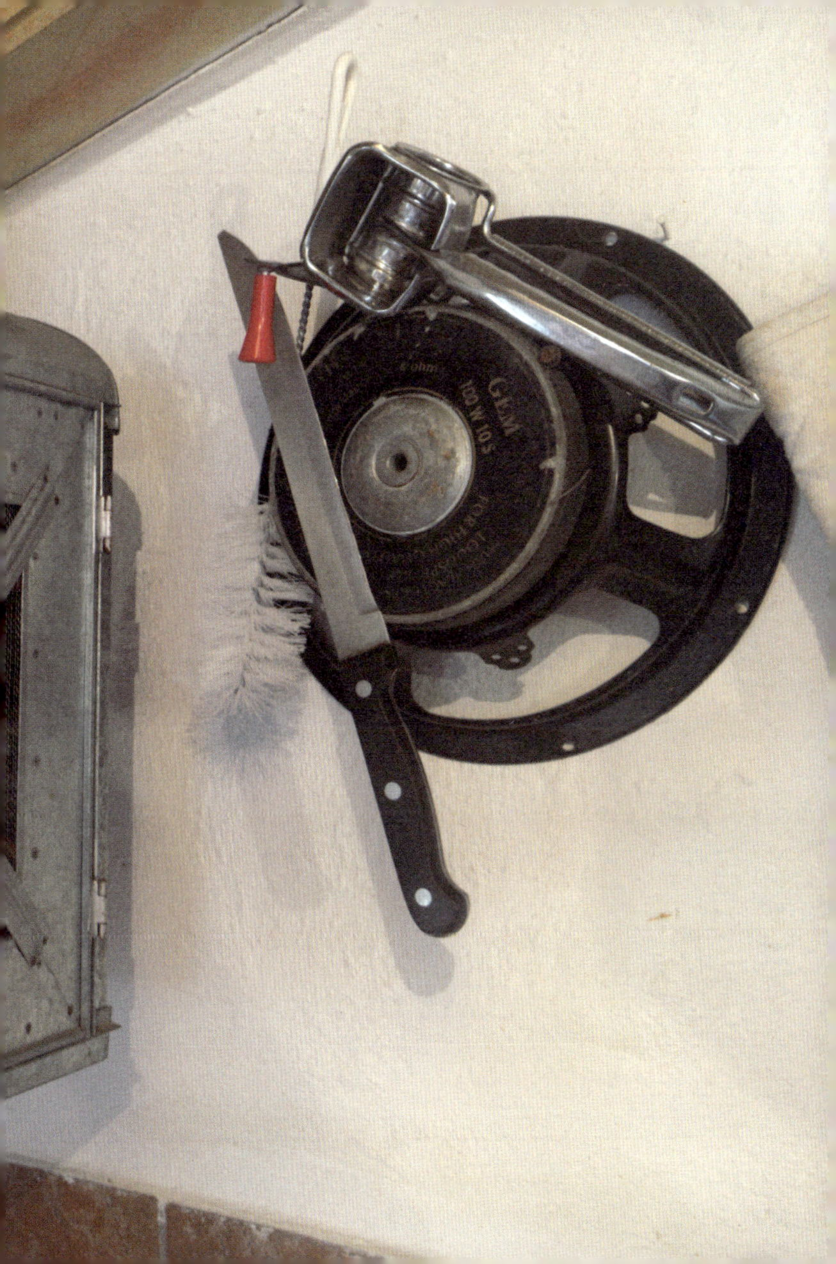

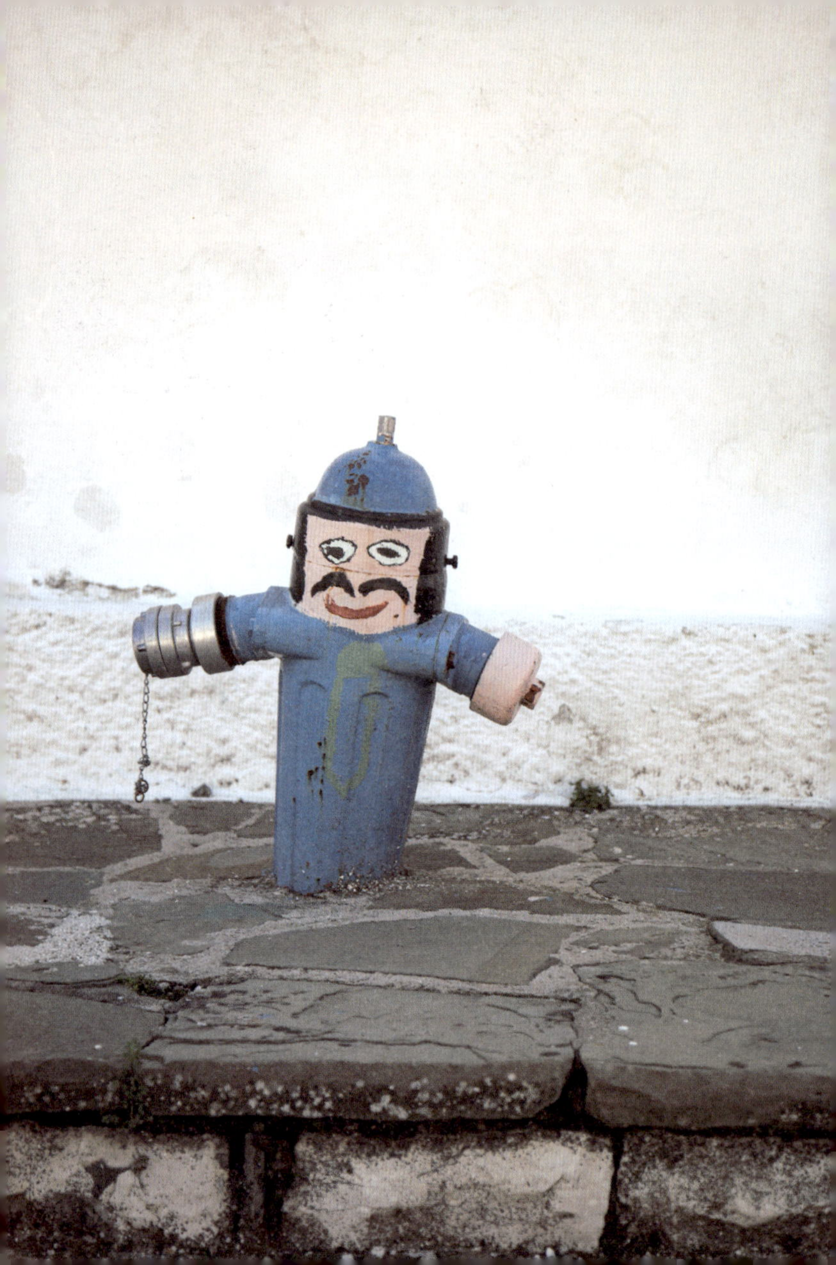

Fire hydrant decoration
Paint

Ioannina
Manos Chatzikonstantis

Planters
Feta cheese tin containers

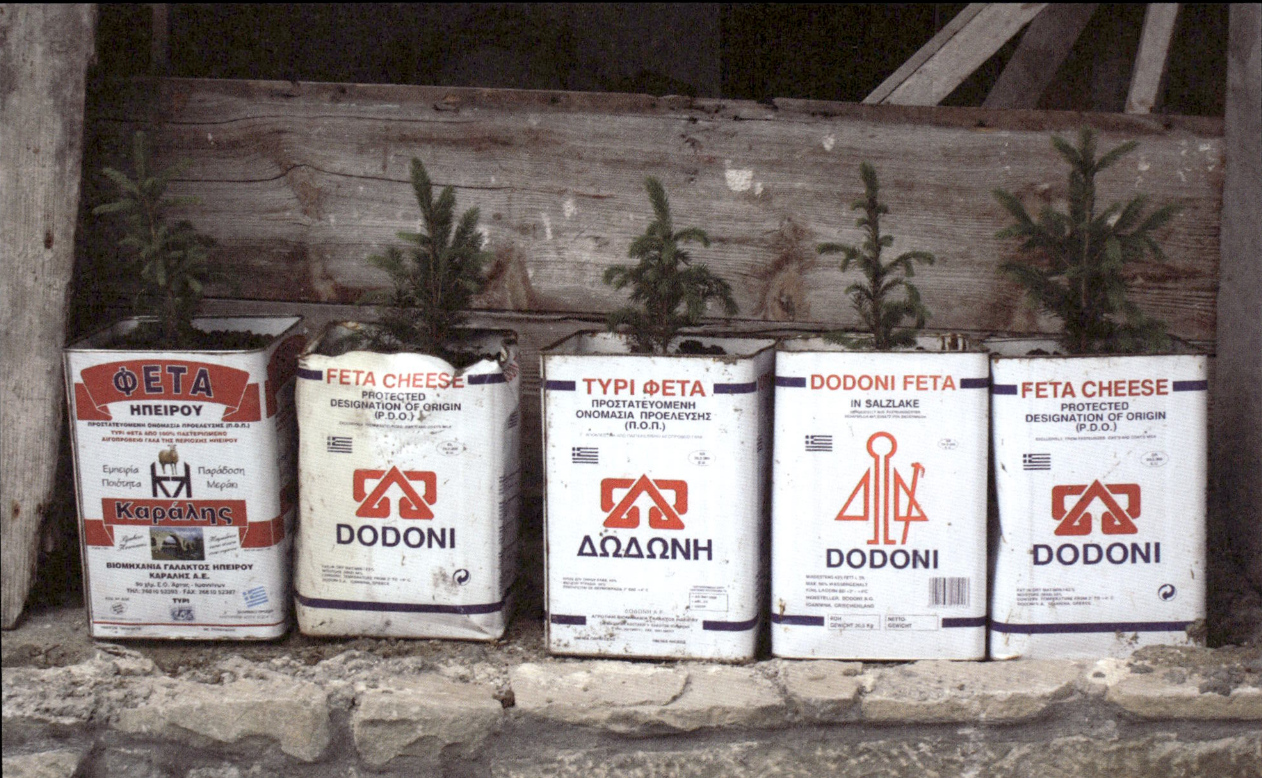
ΦΕΤΑ
ΗΠΕΙΡΟΥ
ΠΡΟΣΤΑΤΕΥΟΜΕΝΗ ΟΝΟΜΑΣΙΑ ΠΡΟΕΛΕΥΣΗΣ (Π.Ο.Π.)
Εμπειρία
Ποιότητα
Παράδοση
Μεράκι
Καράλης
ΒΙΟΜΗΧΑΝΙΑ ΓΑΛΑΚΤΟΣ ΗΠΕΙΡΟΥ
ΚΑΡΑΛΗΣ Α.Ε.
FETA CHEESE
PROTECTED
DESIGNATION OF ORIGIN
(P.D.O.)
DODONI
ΤΥΡΙ ΦΕΤΑ
ΠΡΟΣΤΑΤΕΥΟΜΕΝΗ
ΟΝΟΜΑΣΙΑ ΠΡΟΕΛΕΥΣΗΣ
(Π.Ο.Π.)
ΔΩΔΩΝΗ
DODONI FETA
IN SALZLAKE
DODONI
FETA CHEESE
PROTECTED
DESIGNATION OF ORIGIN
(P.D.O.)
DODONI

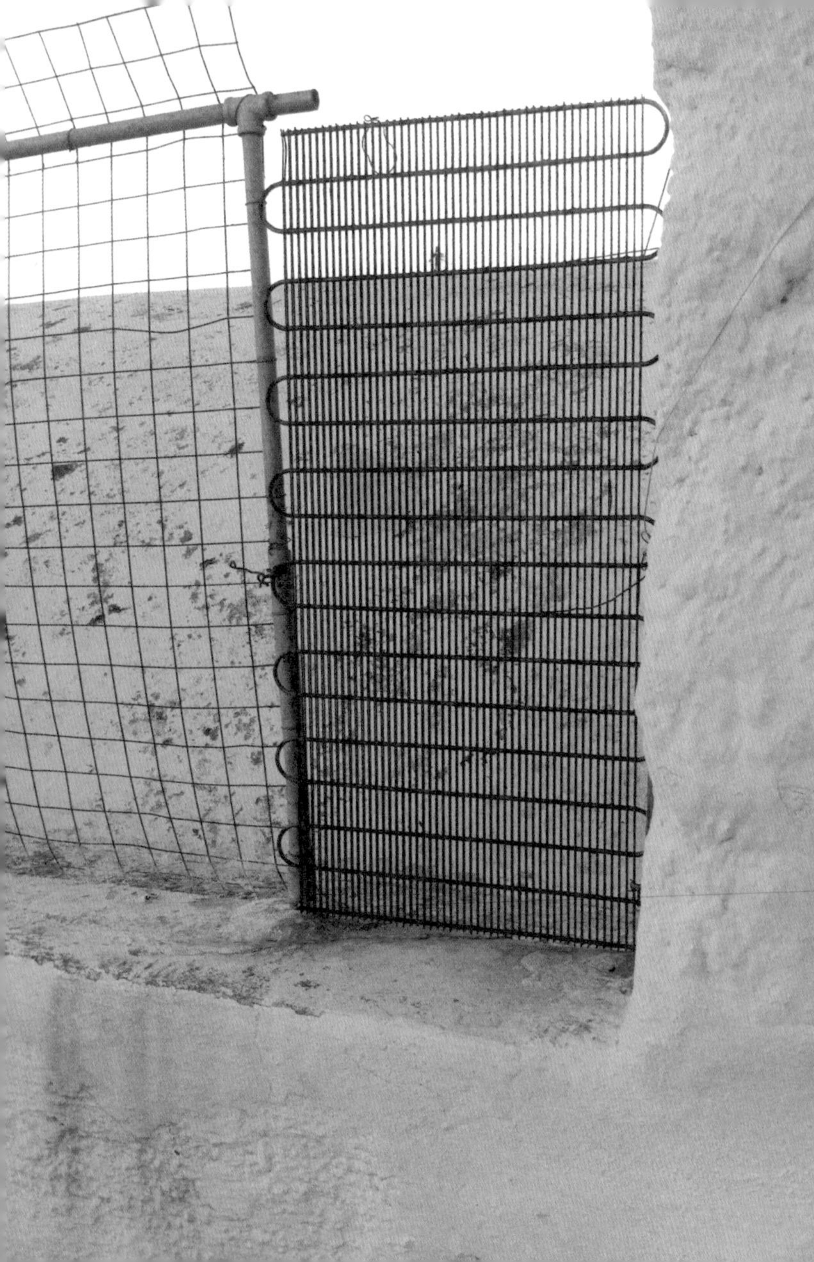

Courtyard gate

Tubes, wire, refrigeration resistors

Sunshade

4L Renault bonnet, steel bar

People congregate in clubs of thematic interest to discuss, live and develop their common interest. Often, they put work into making sure that their club communicates its values, be it branding, installations, events etc. Here, in a modified vehicles' club, this designer has used a car bonnet to protect the entrance of the club's premises from the elements.

Koropi
Yorgos Fakinos

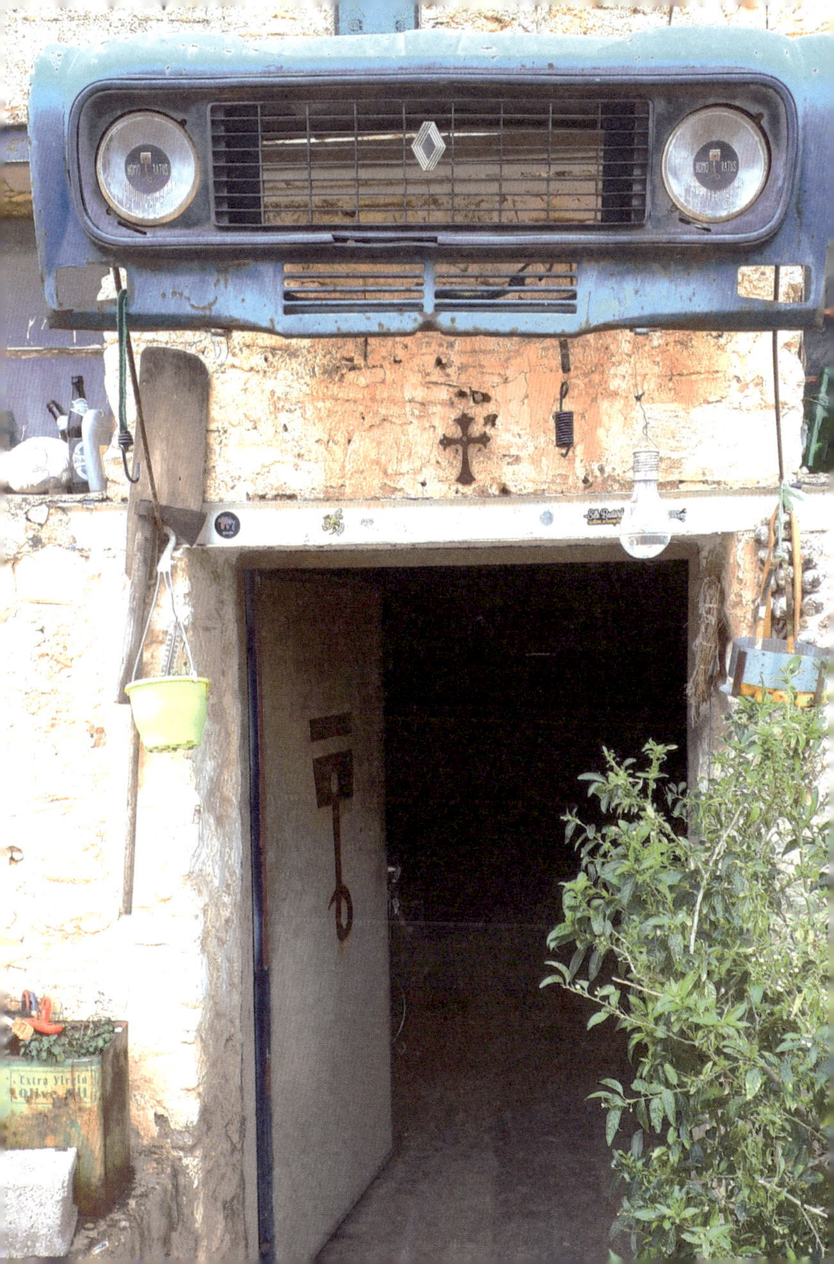

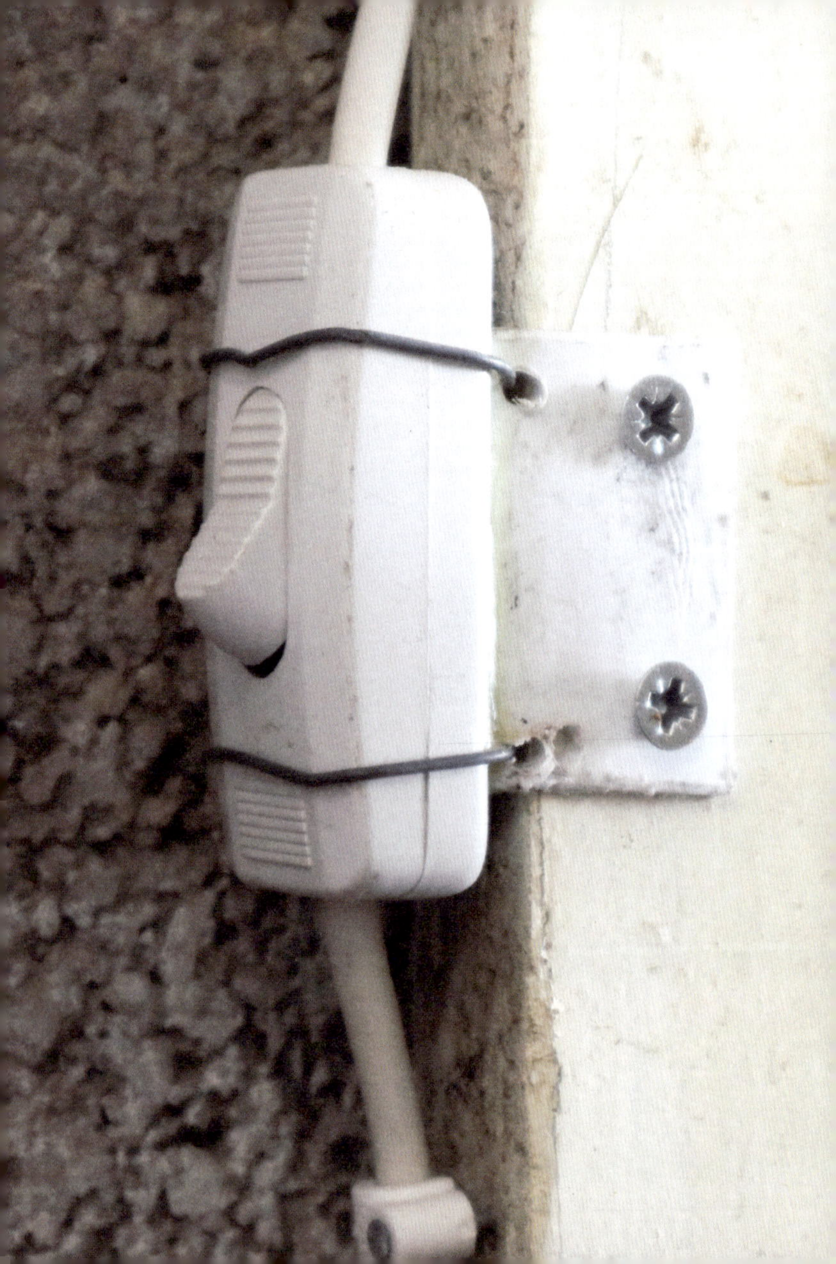

Wall-mounted light switch
Wire, plastic bracket, screws

Nea Moudania
Maria & Prodromos Minaoglou

Planters

Sisterns, screws, metal brackets

The centre of Athens has been so densely built that green spaces are limited and parks not as widespread as in other European capitals. This DIY designer uses cisterns that once held water to now hold fertile soil for growing plants on the street.

Athens
Kanella Arapoglou

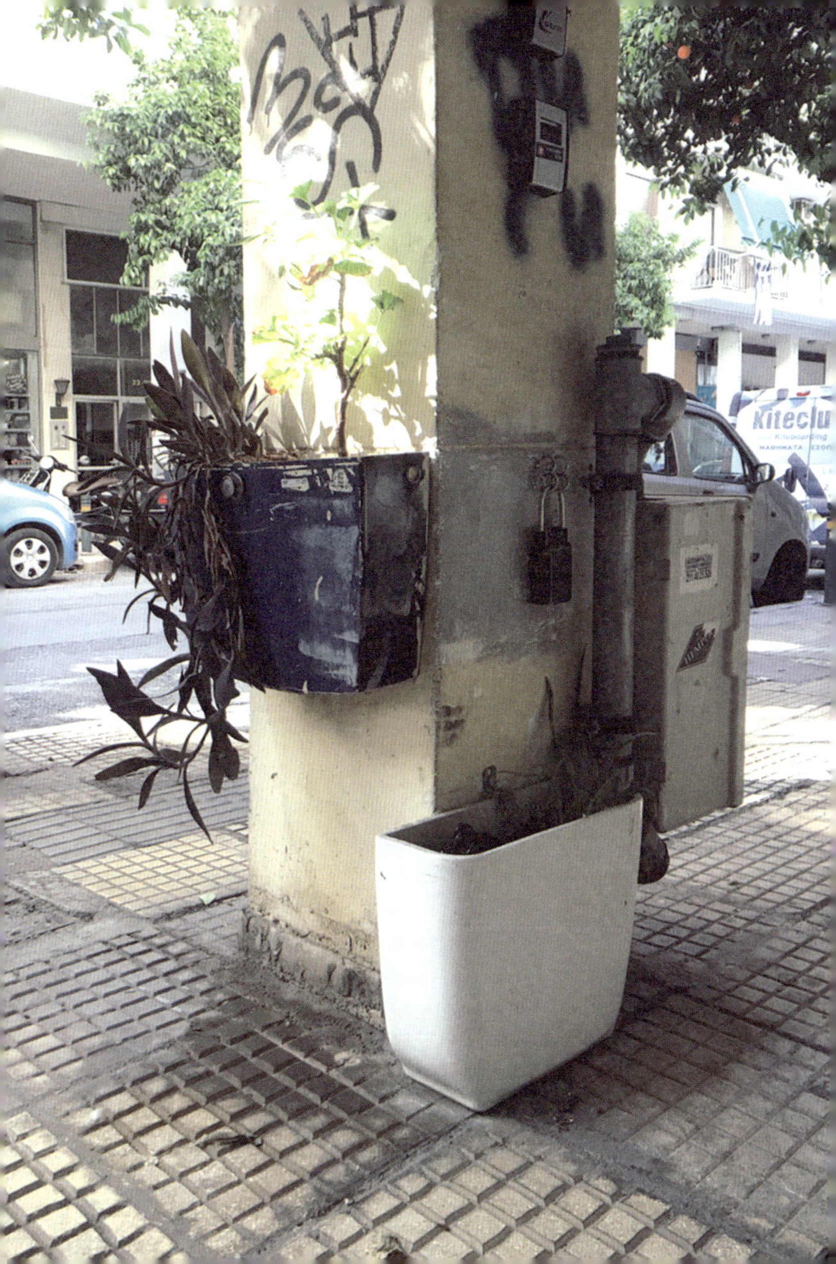
Kiteclu

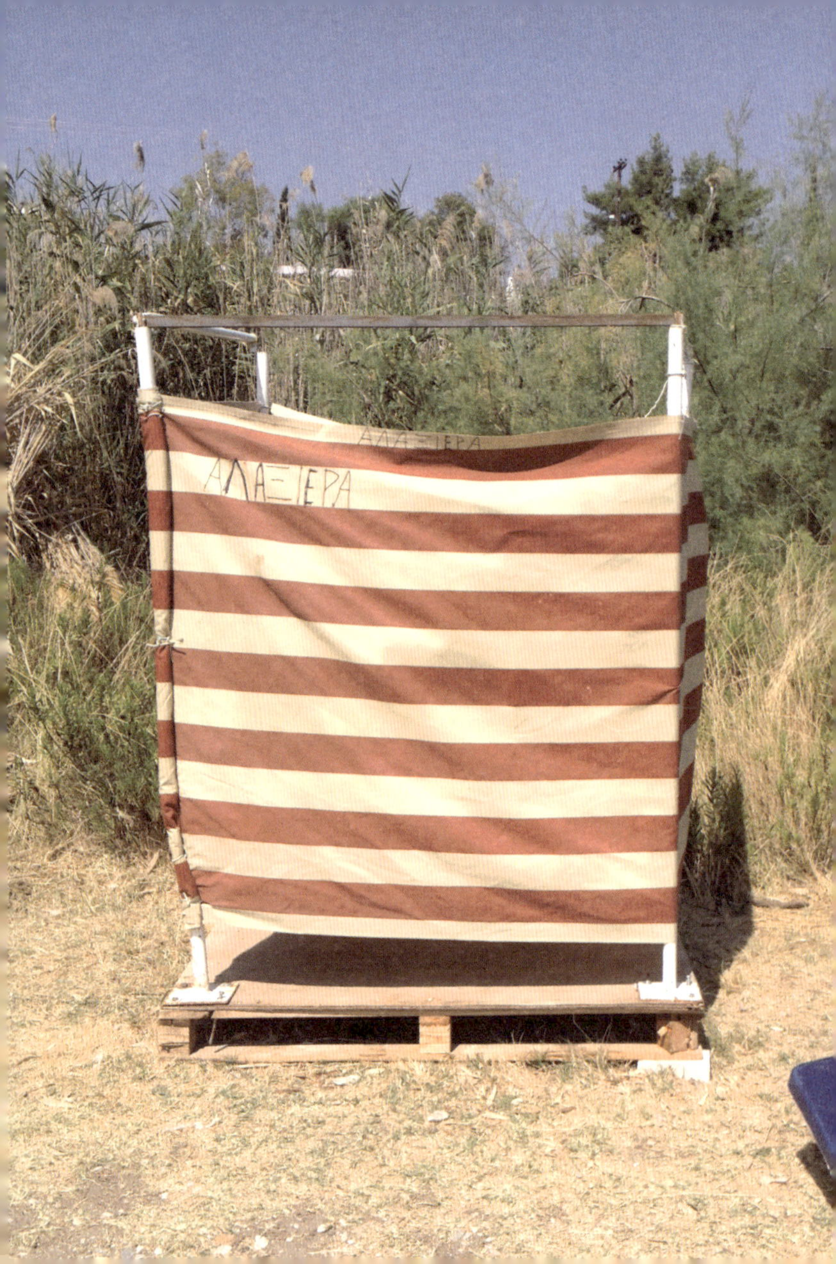
ΑΛΛΑΞΙΕΡΑ
ΑΛΛΑΞΙΕΡΑ

Beach changing room

Tarpaulin, aluminium, wood planks, MDF

Shading system

Beach umbrella, rope

Syros

Sotiris Patronis

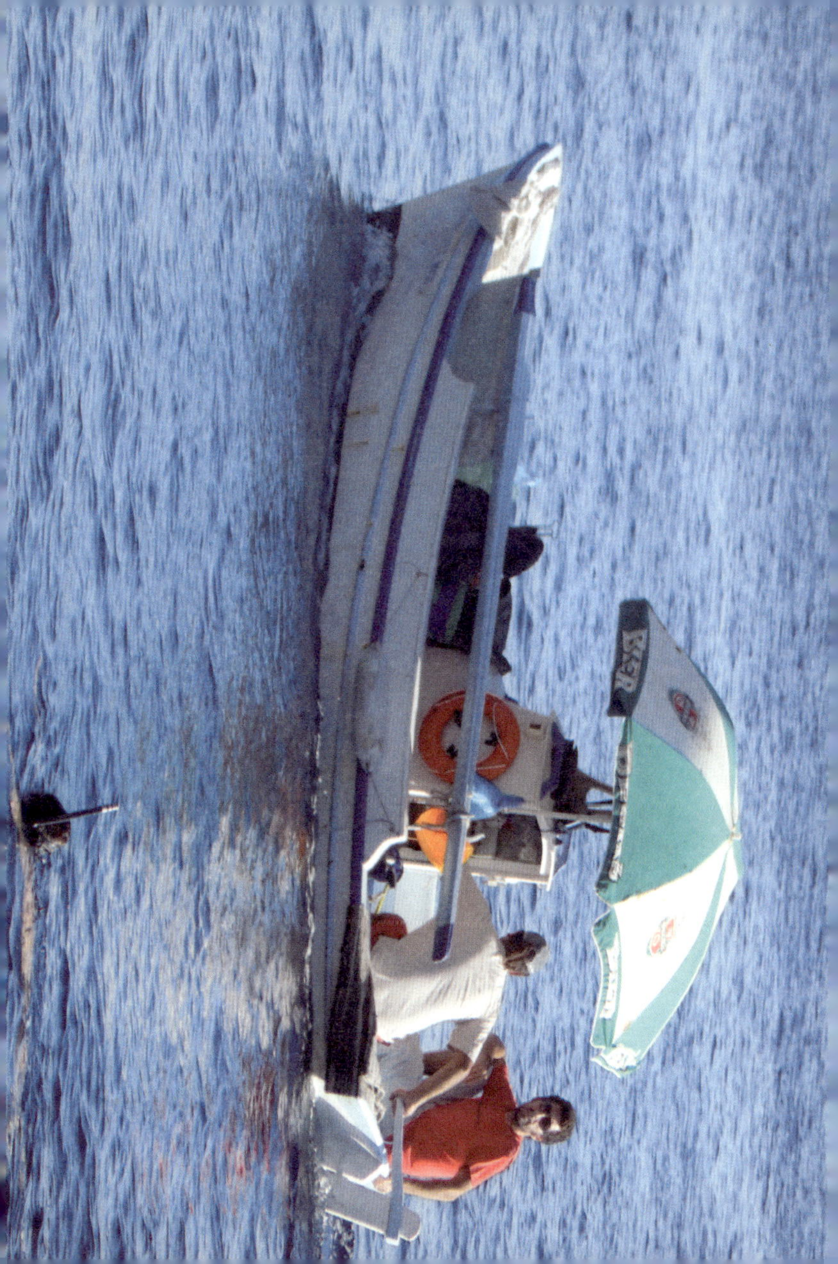

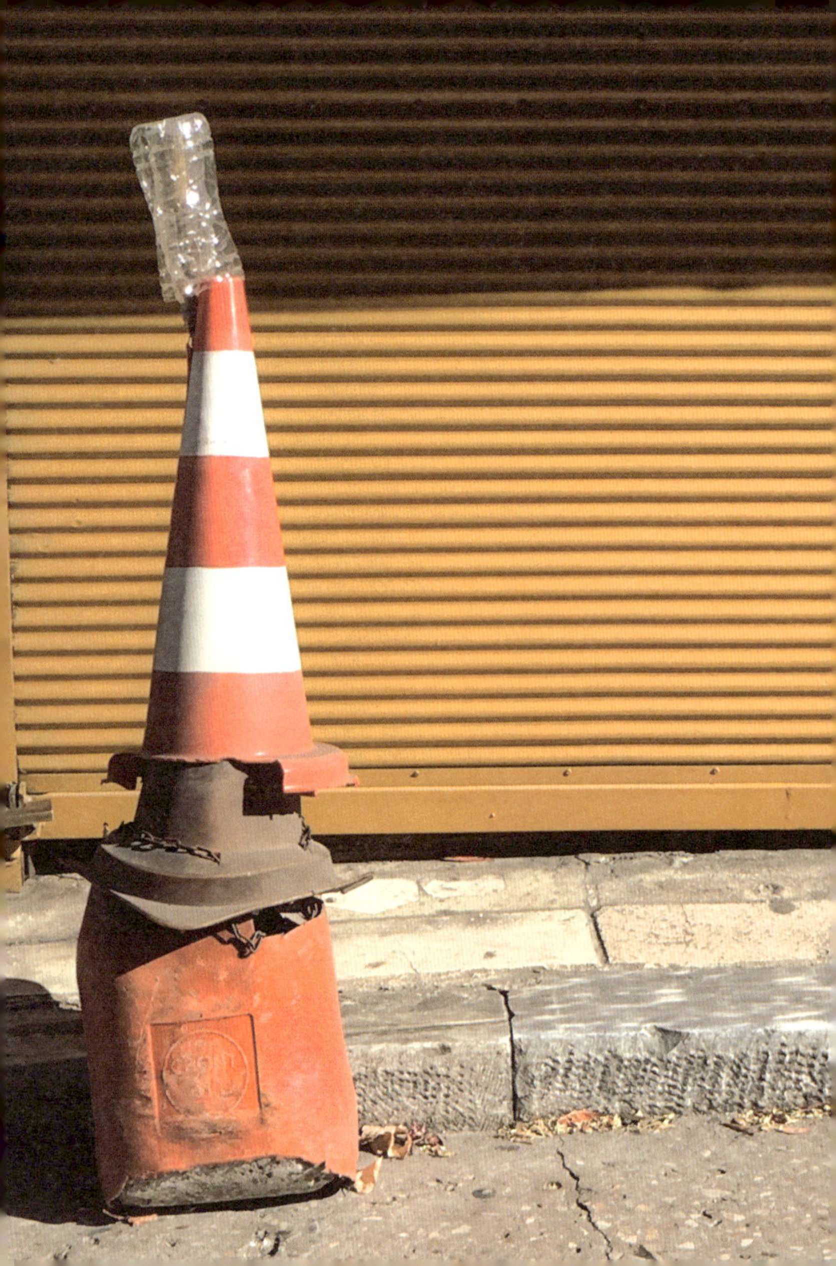

Parking spot holder

Plastic cones, barrel, plastic water bottle, concrete

Athens
Papairlines

Donation box
Plastic water bottle, carton, pen

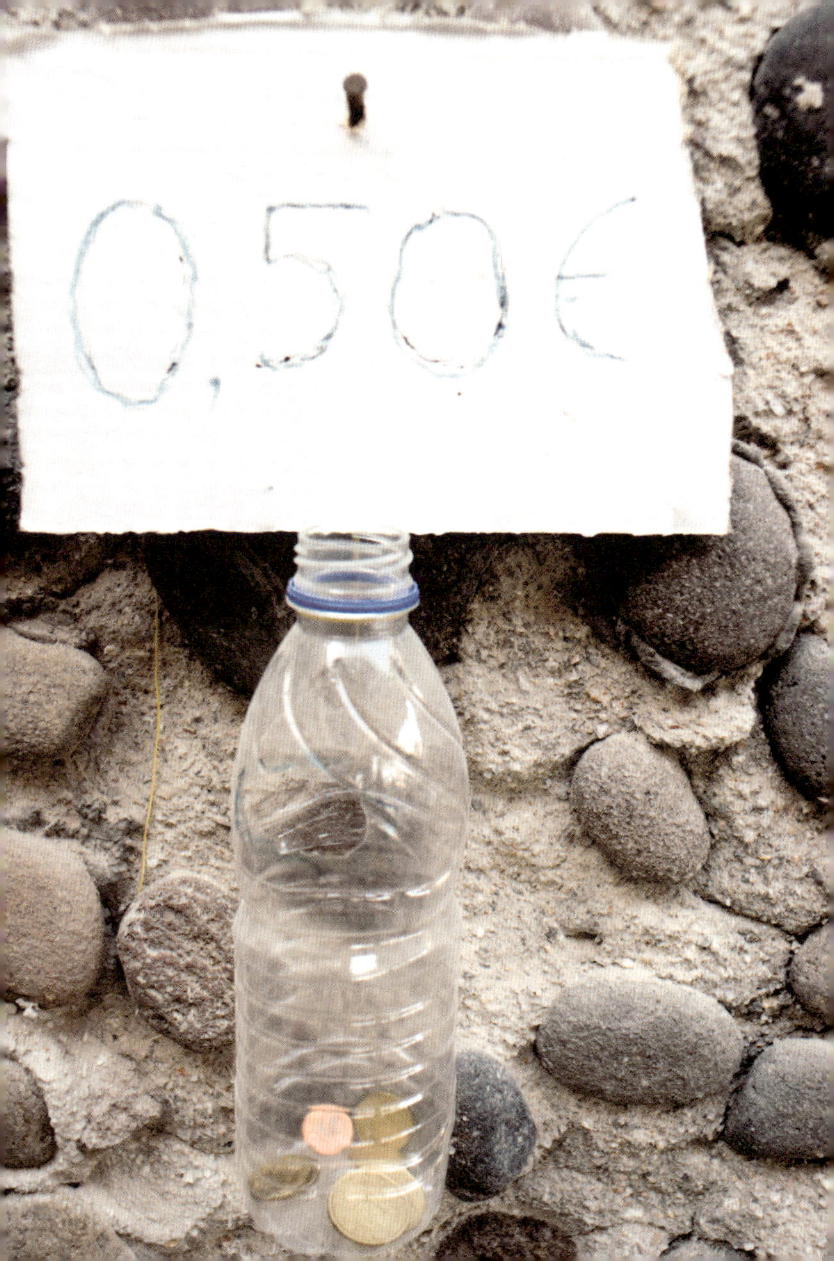
0,50€

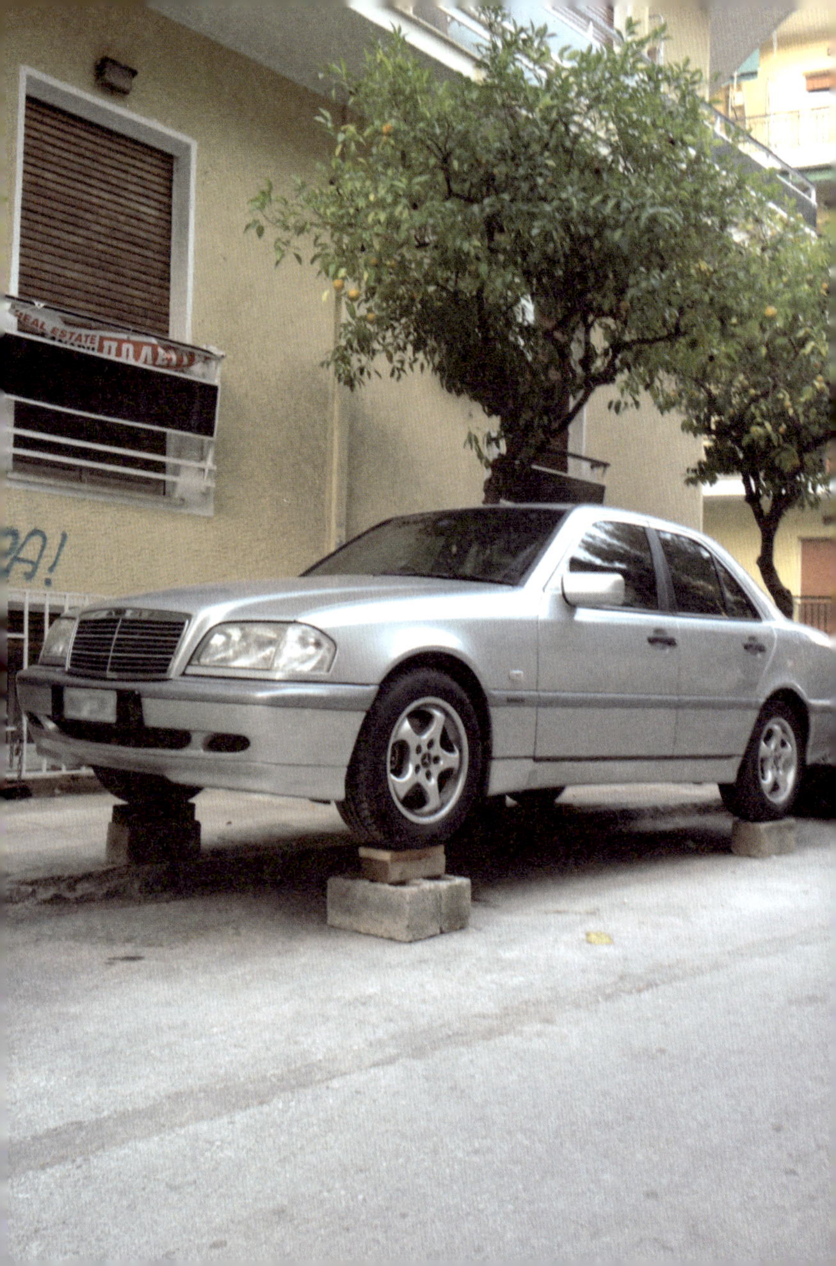

We cannot understand why this is happening, but this car has been on and off the ground in this way for many years.
If you have any clue or information, please contact us.

Speed limit sign
Straw bales, spray paint

Agrinio
Sotiris Patronis

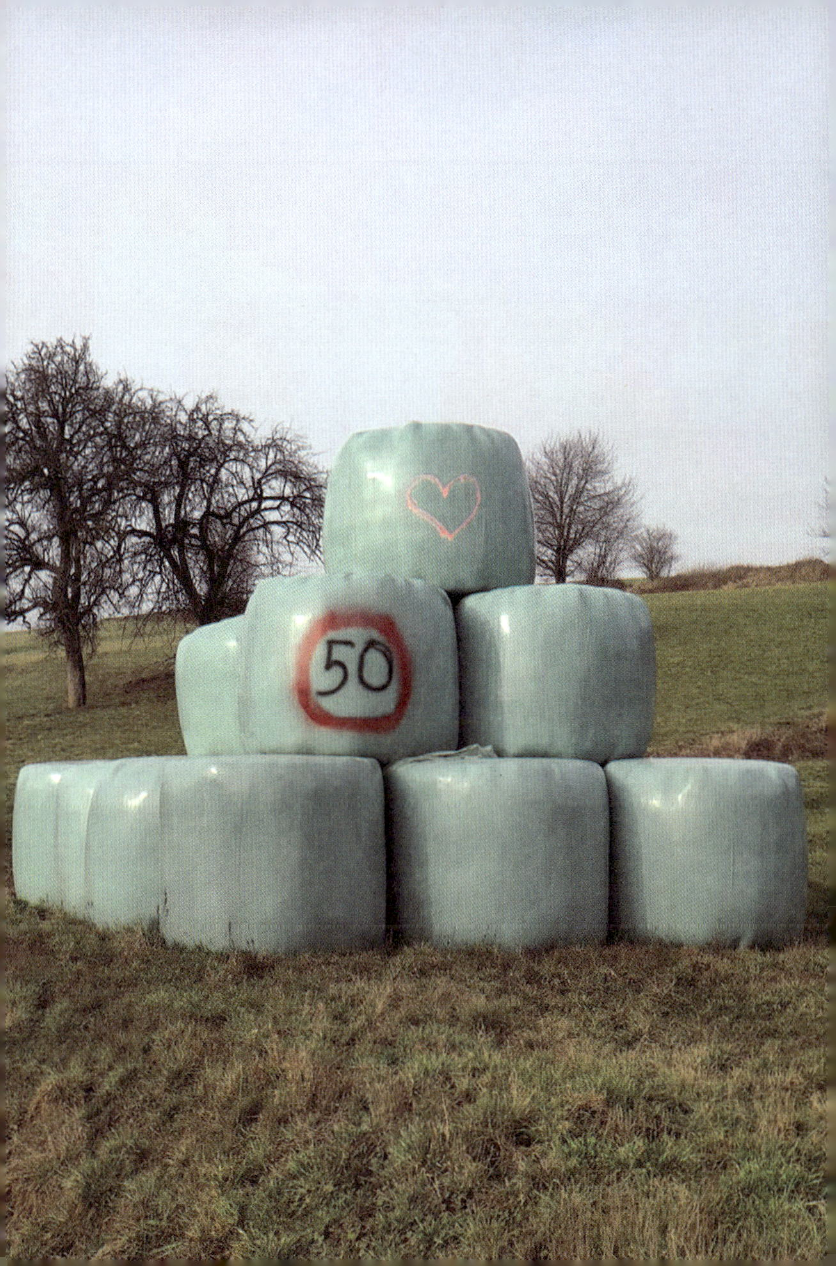
50

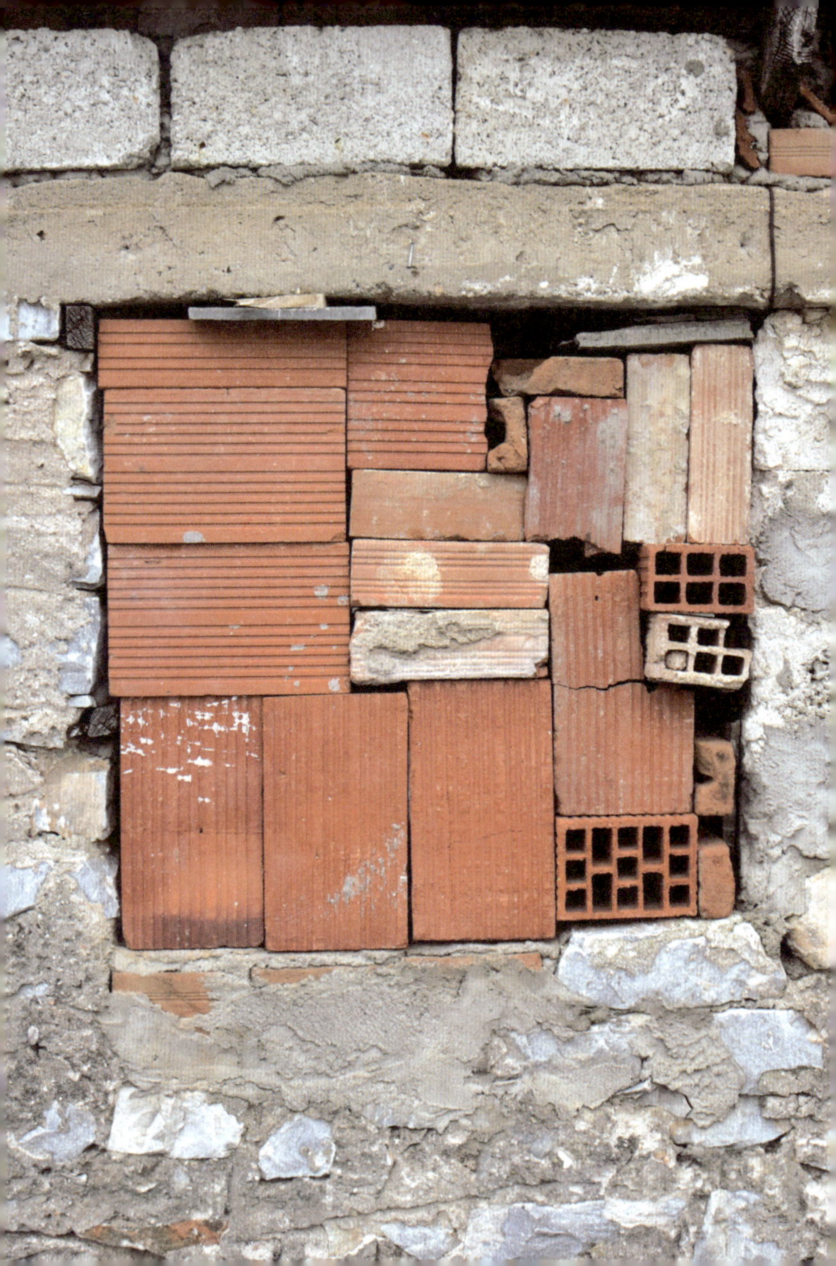

Window blocker

Bricks in various dimensions, ceramic & stone tiles

Petroussa

 Vasilios Kiratsis, Kiriaki Aidinli, Lazaros Firtikiadis

Spoon
Driftwood, seashell

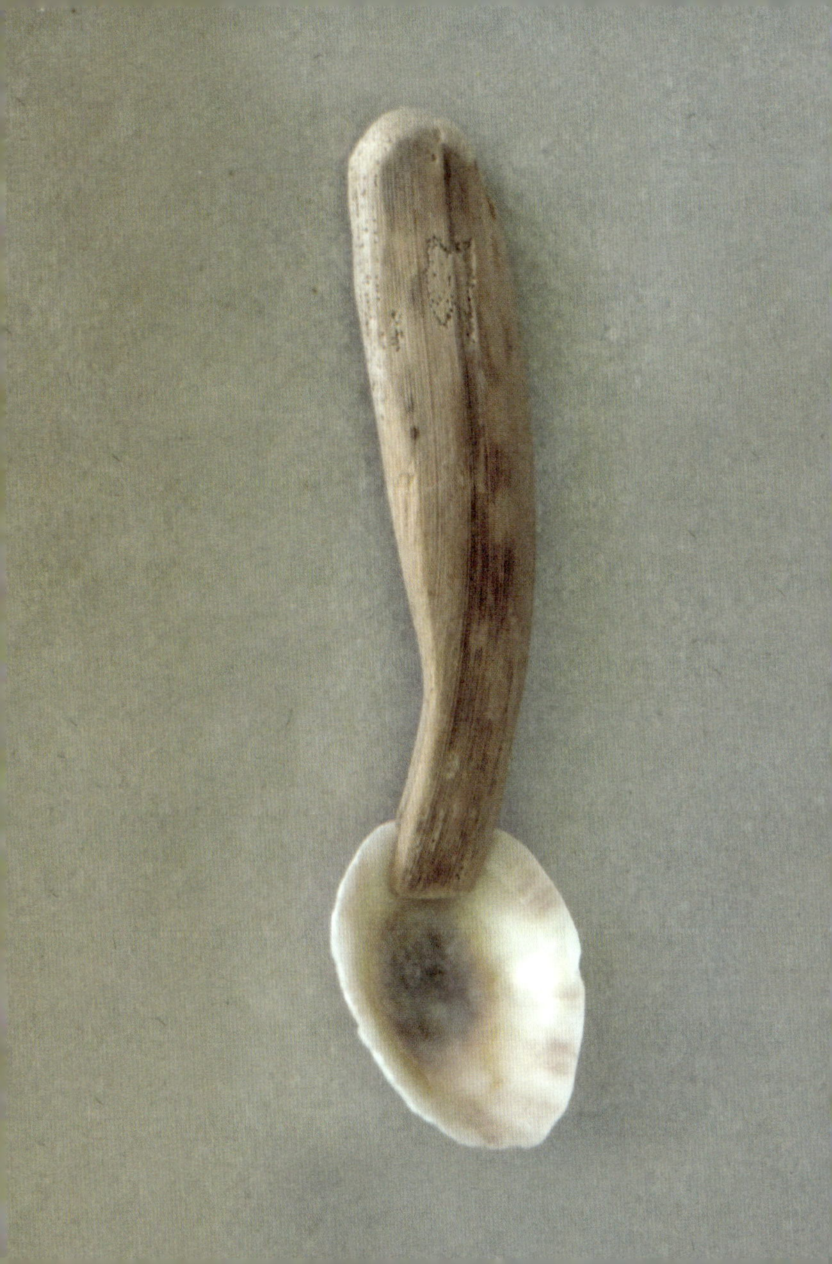

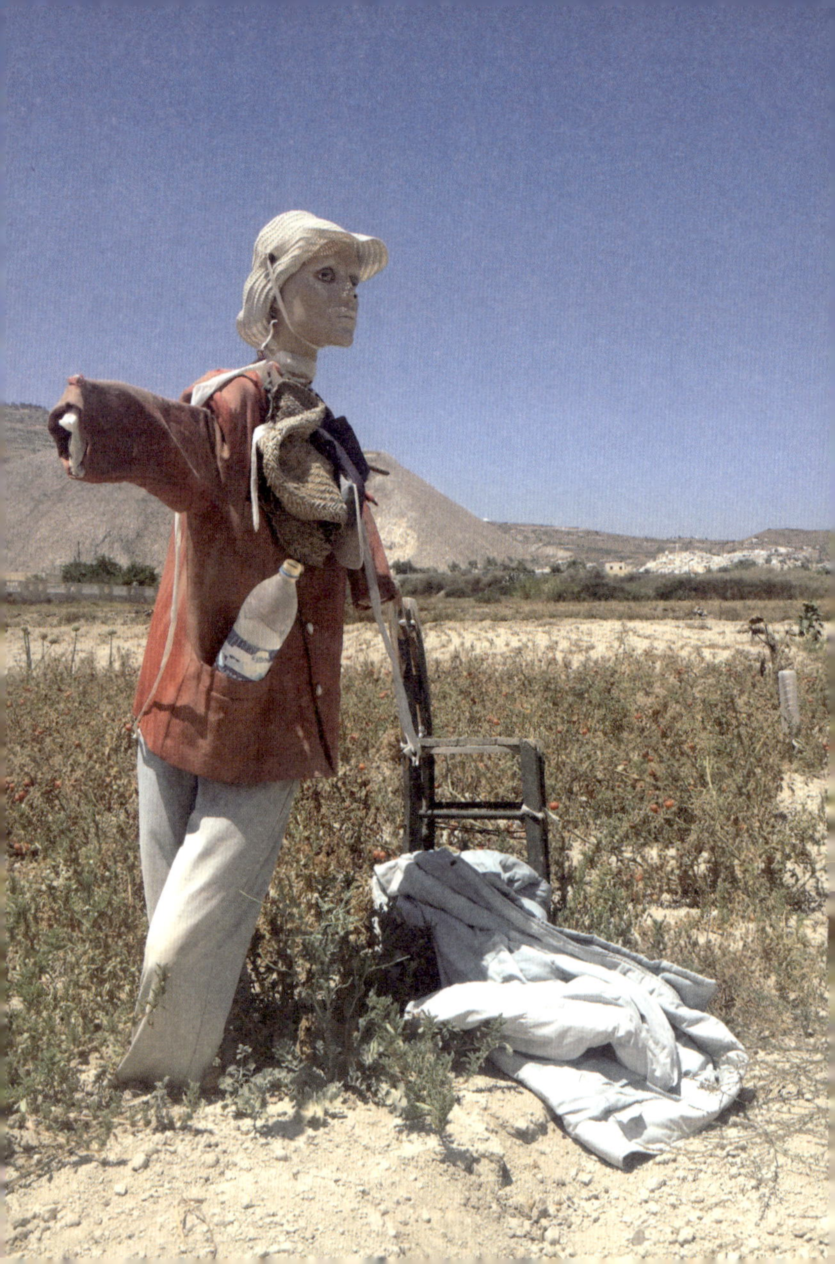

Scarecrow

Mannequin, old clothes, chair

Santorini

Papairlines

Sunshade
Thatched hat

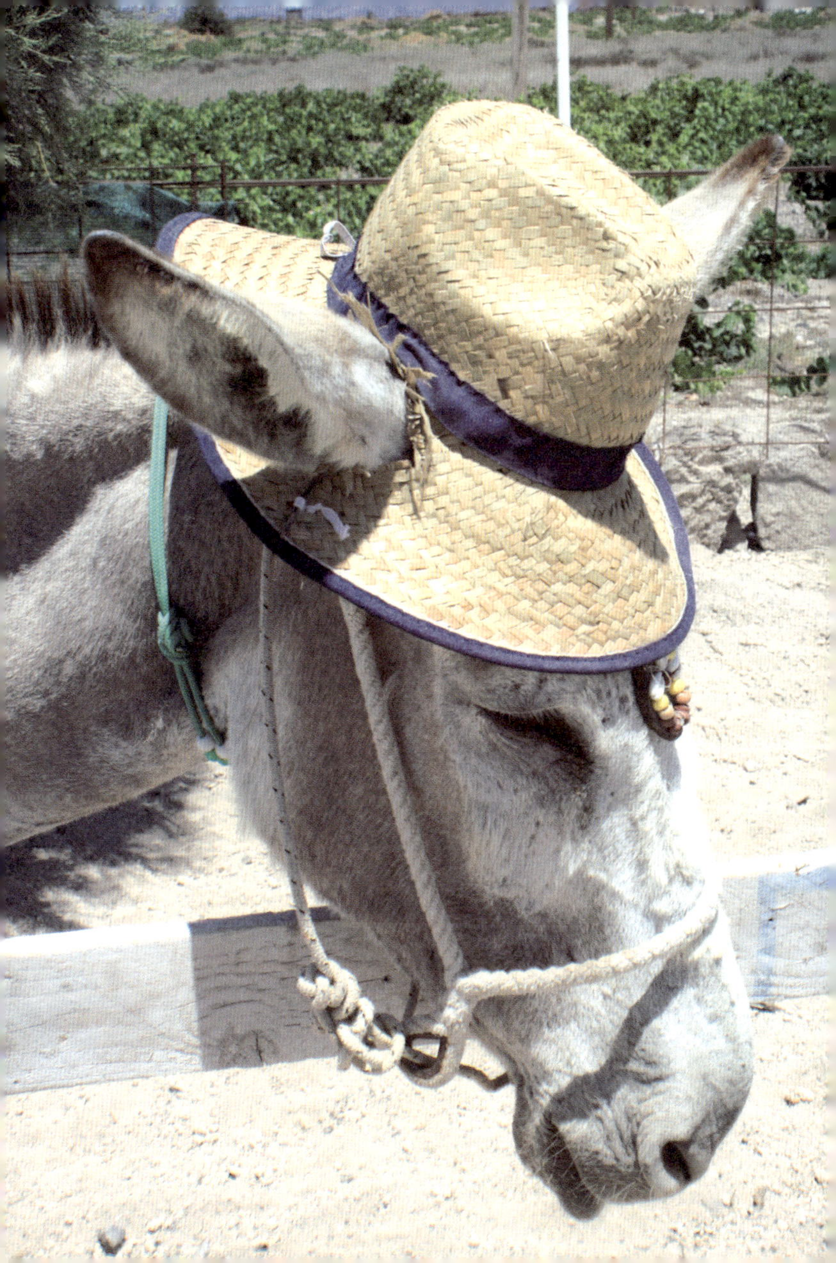

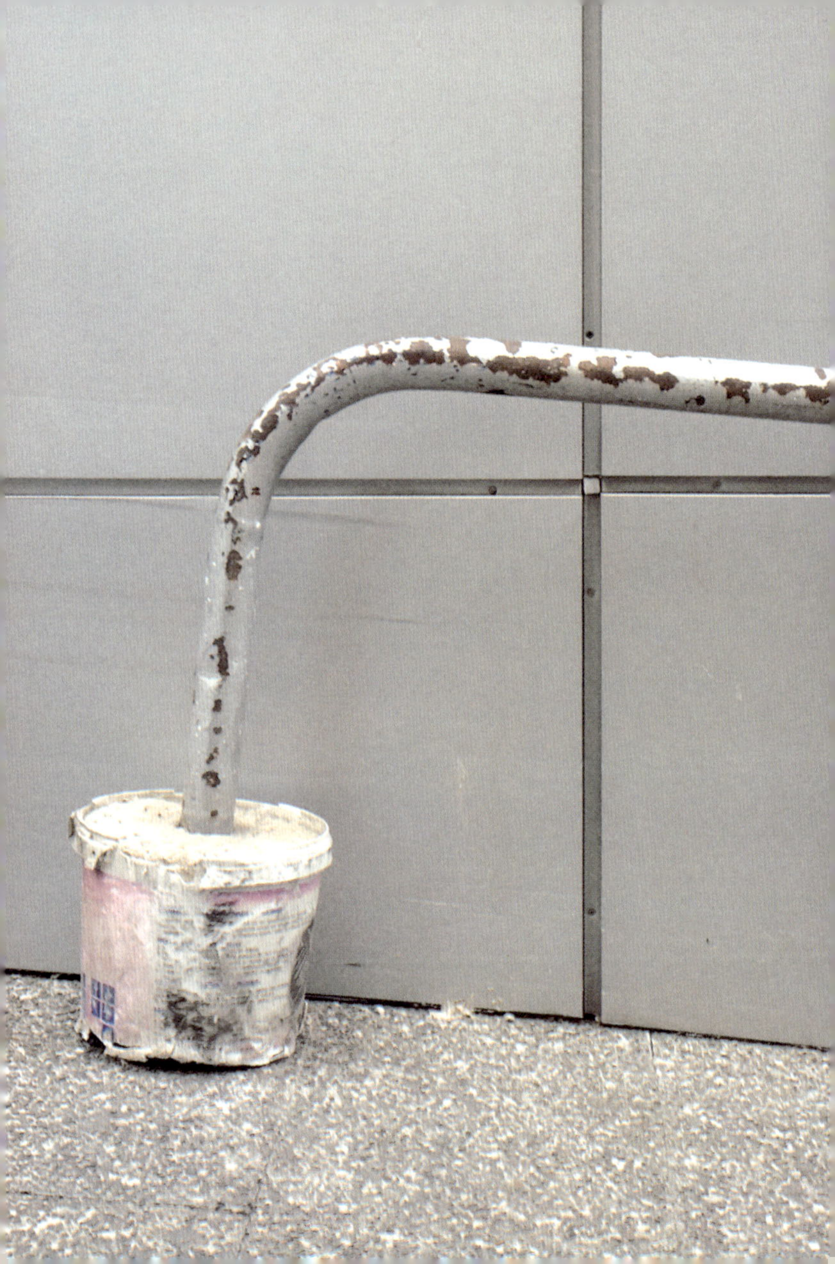

Concrete, plastic paint bucket, metal pipe

In Athens city center, car parking is limited. And while citizens and residents can use public transport, some businesses require vehicles to carry out their services but do not have designated parking spots. Here, a business owner has created a mobile parking reservation device which informally serves as a space holder for the business's vehicle when it is out and about.

Protective cover
Lightweight fabric, metal wire

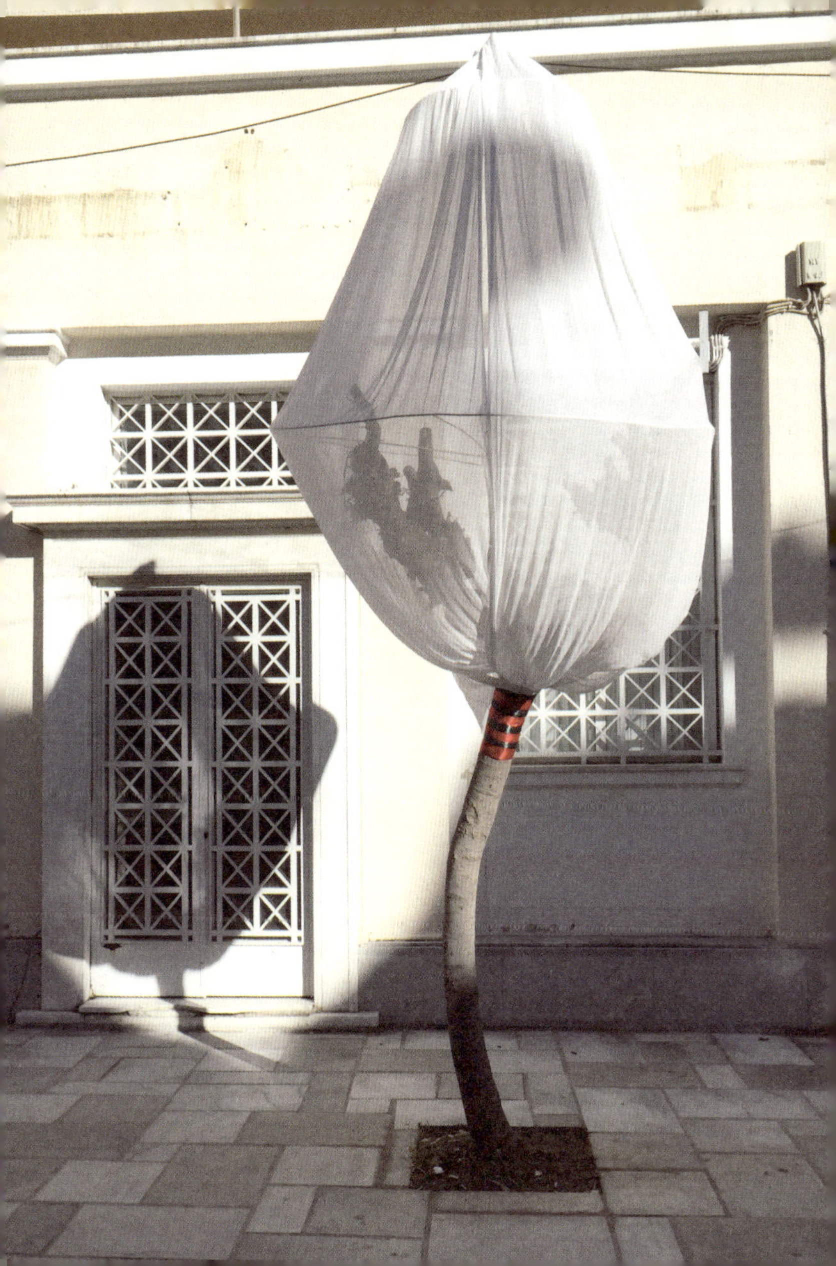

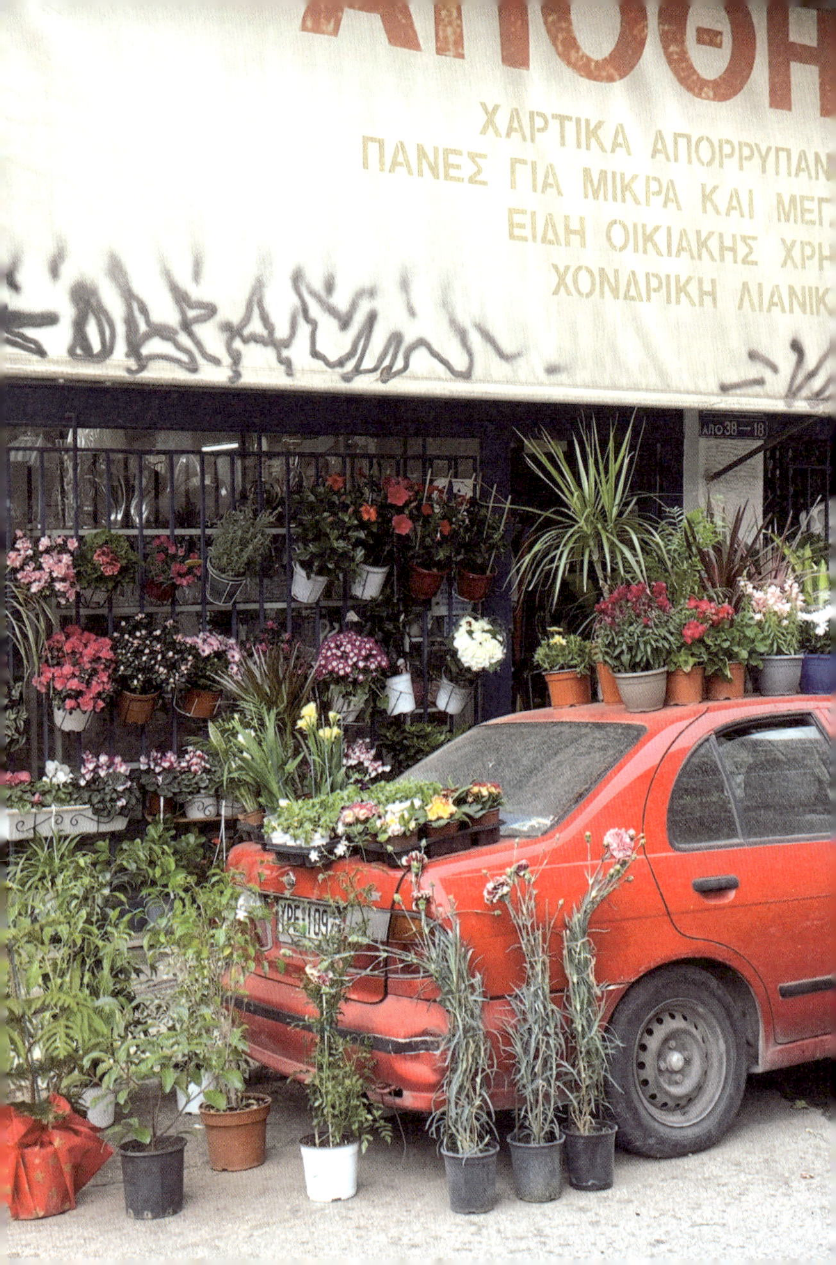
ΧΑΡΤΙΚΑ ΑΠΟΡΡΥΠΑΝ
ΠΑΝΕΣ ΓΙΑ ΜΙΚΡΑ ΚΑΙ ΜΕΓ
ΕΙΔΗ ΟΙΚΙΑΚΗΣ ΧΡΗ
ΧΟΝΔΡΙΚΗ ΛΙΑΝΙΚ

Flower display
Parked car

Athens
Nina Gry Myschetzky

Water tap decoration
Expired parking ticket

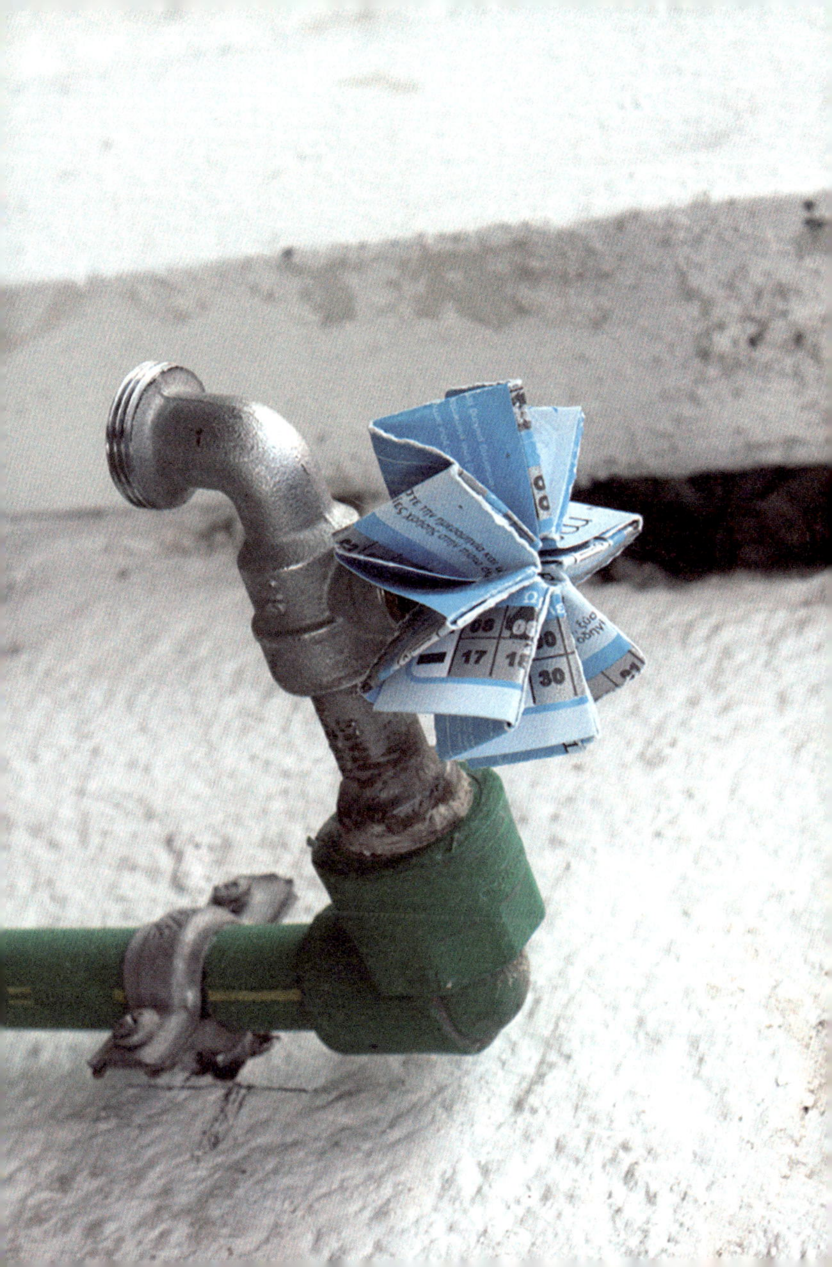

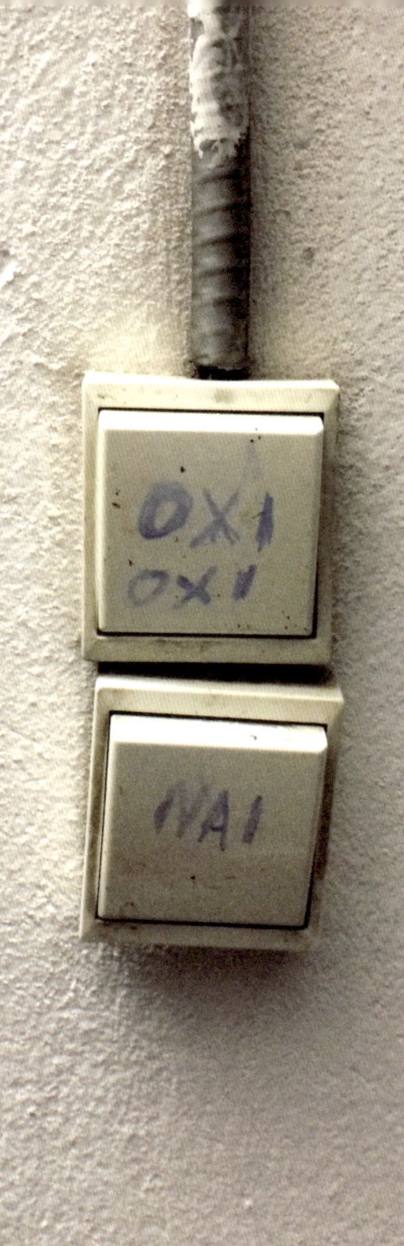
OXI
OXI
NAI

Animal traffic control

Pipe, bearing, wood, wire, metal cans, stones, plastic cone, rope

Modern day shepherds in Greece cannot easily find people to work on their farm. One of the jobs left unstaffed is pushing sheep and goats through a thin passage in order for them to be milked by hand. Here, the rotating device, operated remotely by the shepherd via the pull of a rope (on the left), uses a bright coloured cone and a tin filled with a few stones. Thus, when in use, sheep and goats hear a rattling sound and see waving overhead objects making them push through the passage.

Metsovo
Papairlines

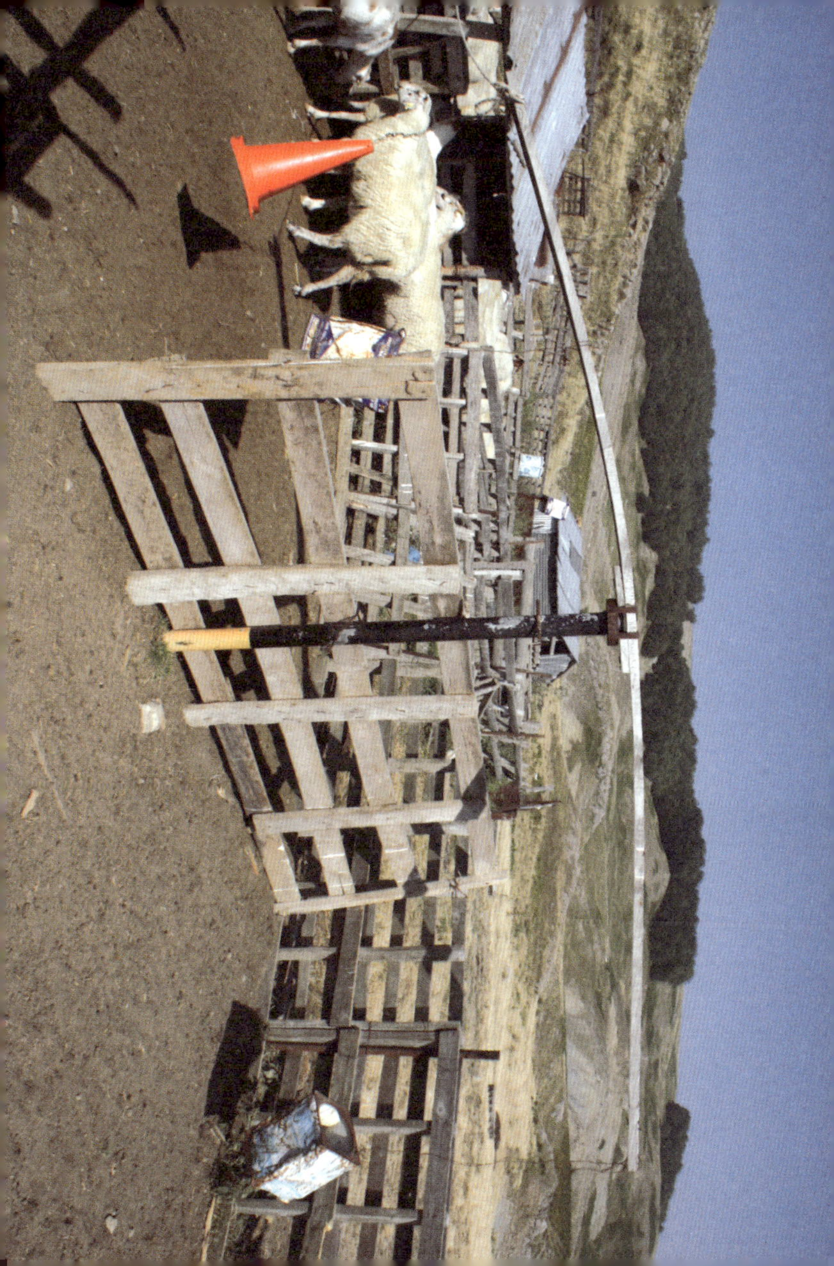

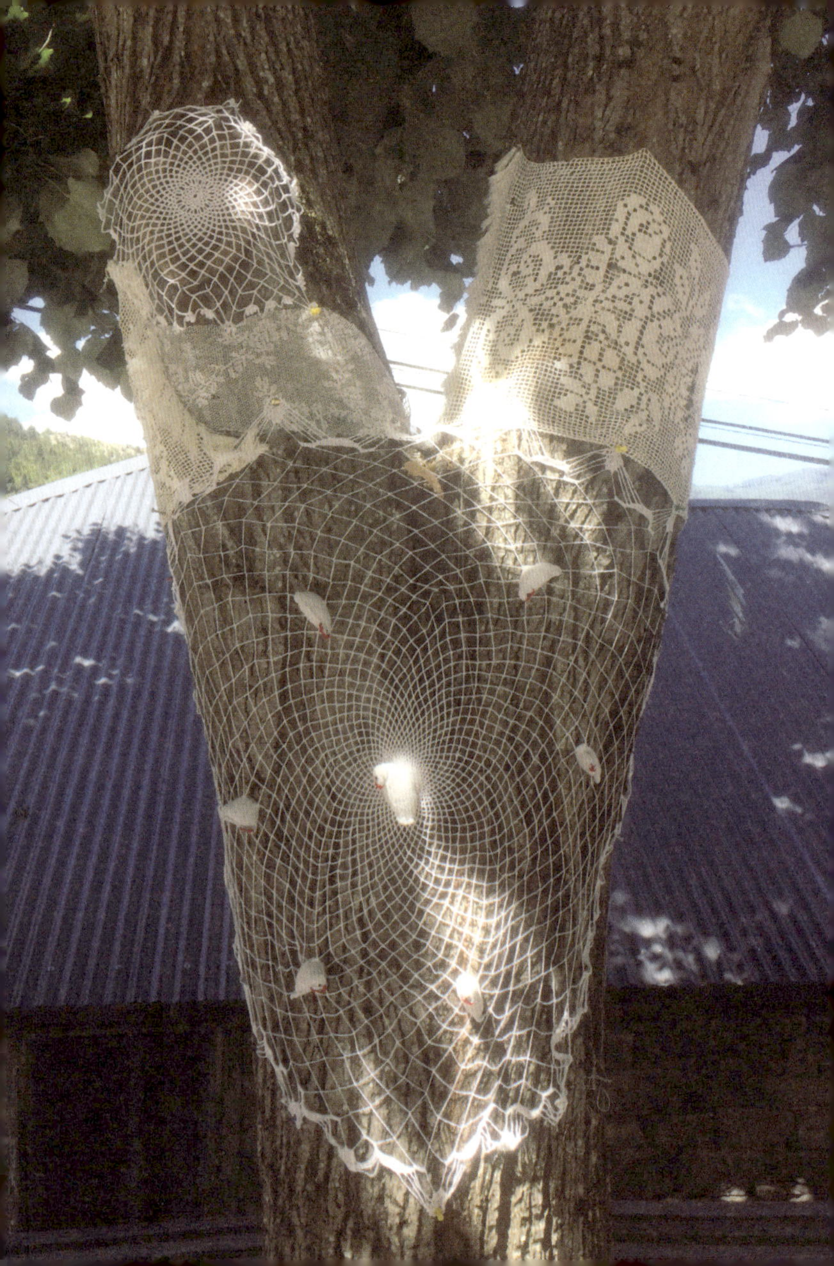

Tree decoration

Thread, crochet, lace

Kastaniani

Papairlines

Public bench
Chairs, reclaimed MDF sheets

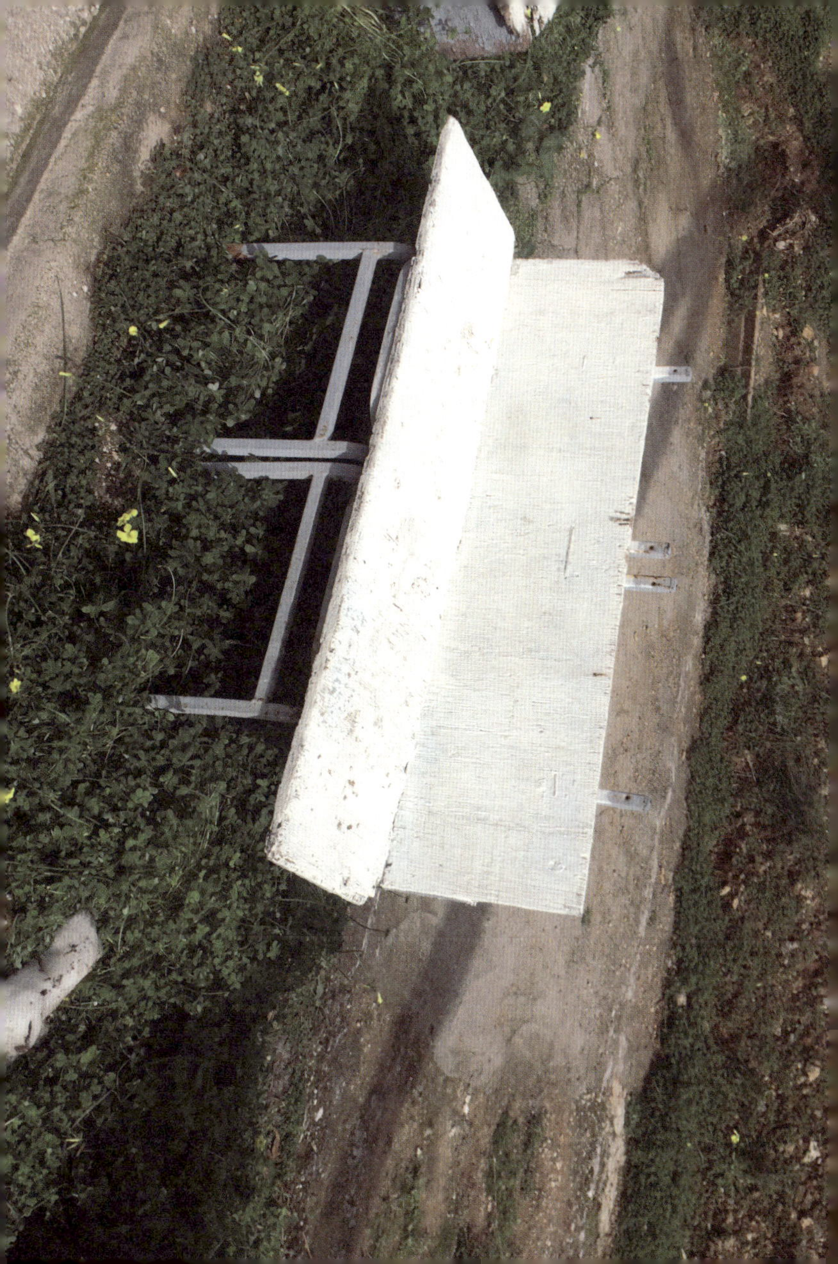

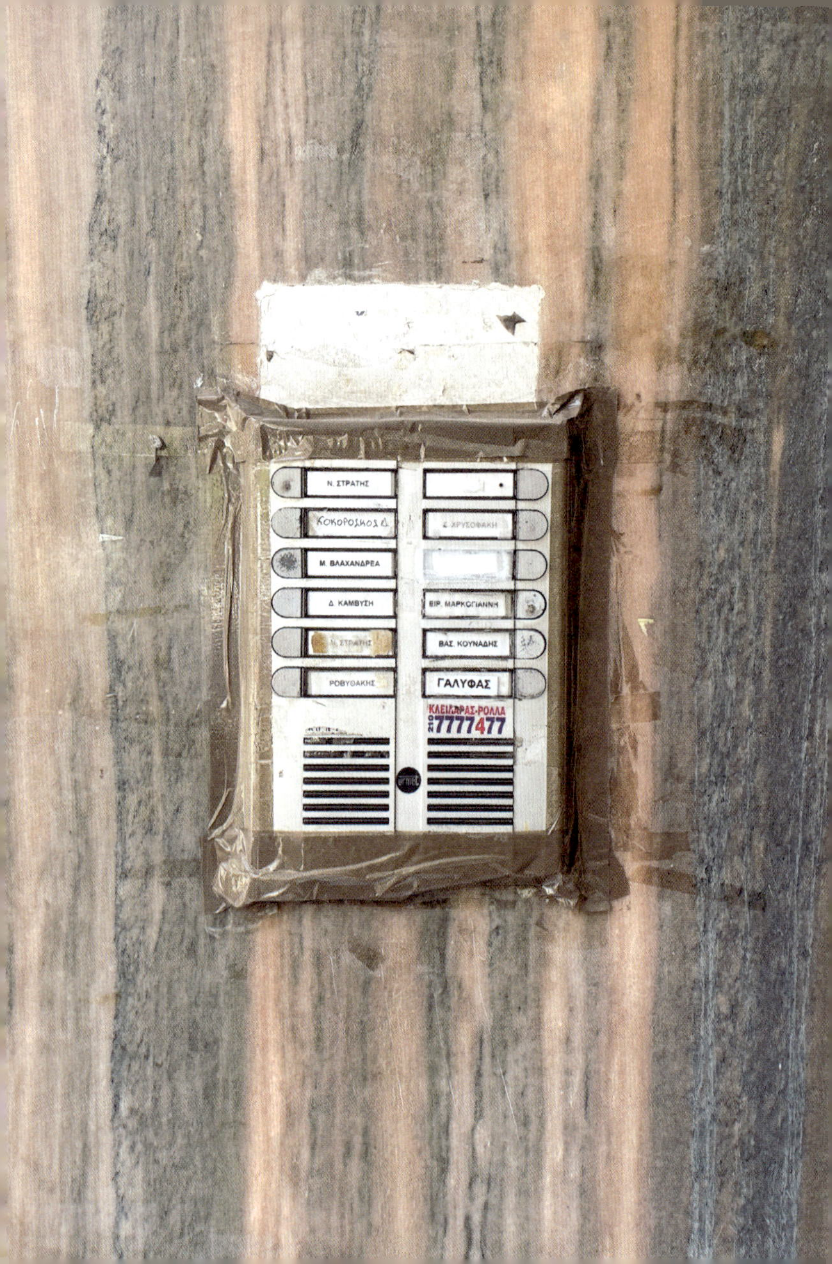

Ν. ΣΤΡΑΤΗΣ
Μ. ΒΛΑΧΑΝΔΡΕΑ
Δ. ΚΑΜΒΥΣΗ
ΡΟΒΥΘΑΚΗΣ
ΒΙΡ. ΜΑΡΚΟΓΙΑΝΝΗ
ΒΑΣ. ΚΟΥΝΑΔΗΣ
ΓΑΛΥΦΑΣ
ΡΟΛΛΑ
210 7777477

Temporary intercom repair
Tape

Athens
Papairlines

Hazard sign
Cardboard box, hazard tape

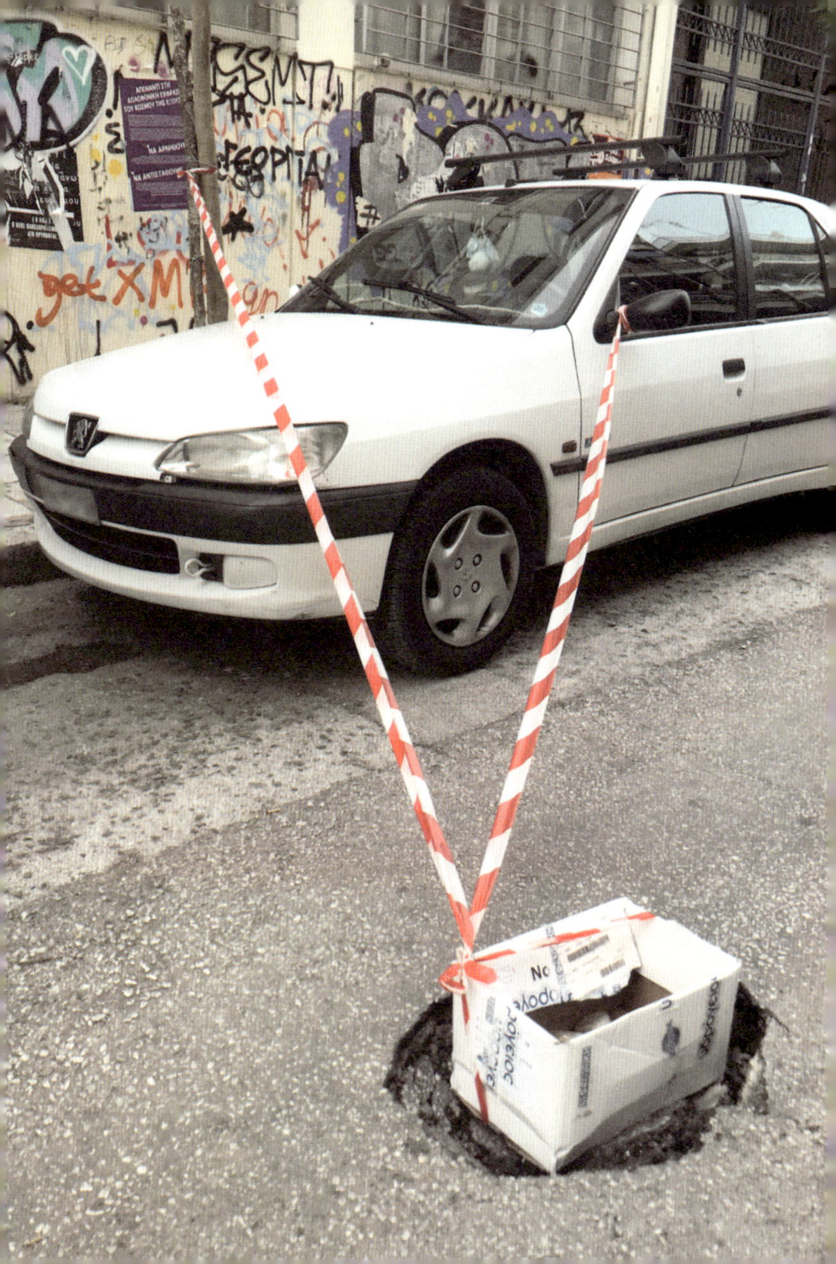
ΑΠΕΝΑΝΤΙ ΣΤΗ
ΤΟΥ ΚΟΣΜΟΥ ΤΗΣ

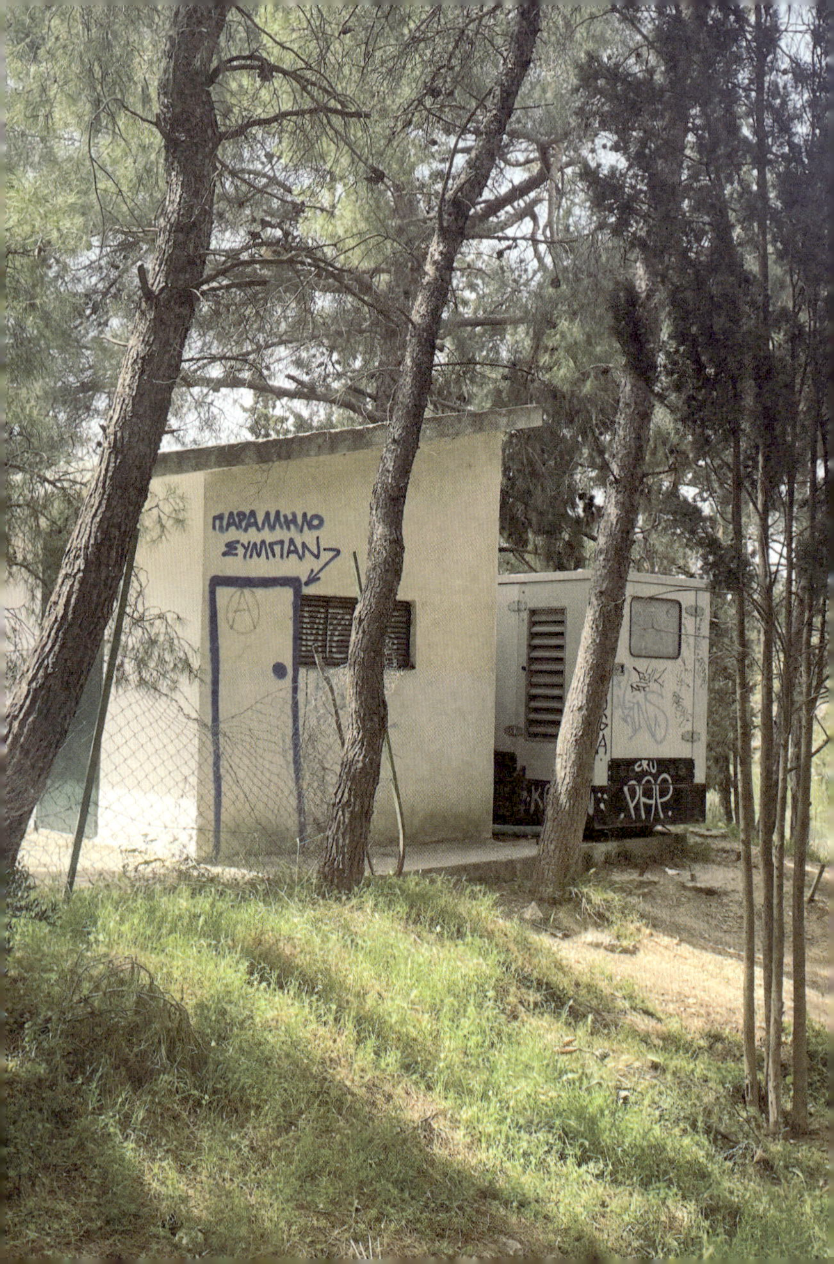
ΠΑΡΑΛΛΗΛΟ
ΣΥΜΠΑΝ
CRU
PAP

Residents of Athens often complain that they live in an unlivable city. This DIY designer took escapism to another level, drawing a door that leads to a parallel universe.

Planters
Used tyres, paint

Kalamos
Sotiris Patronis

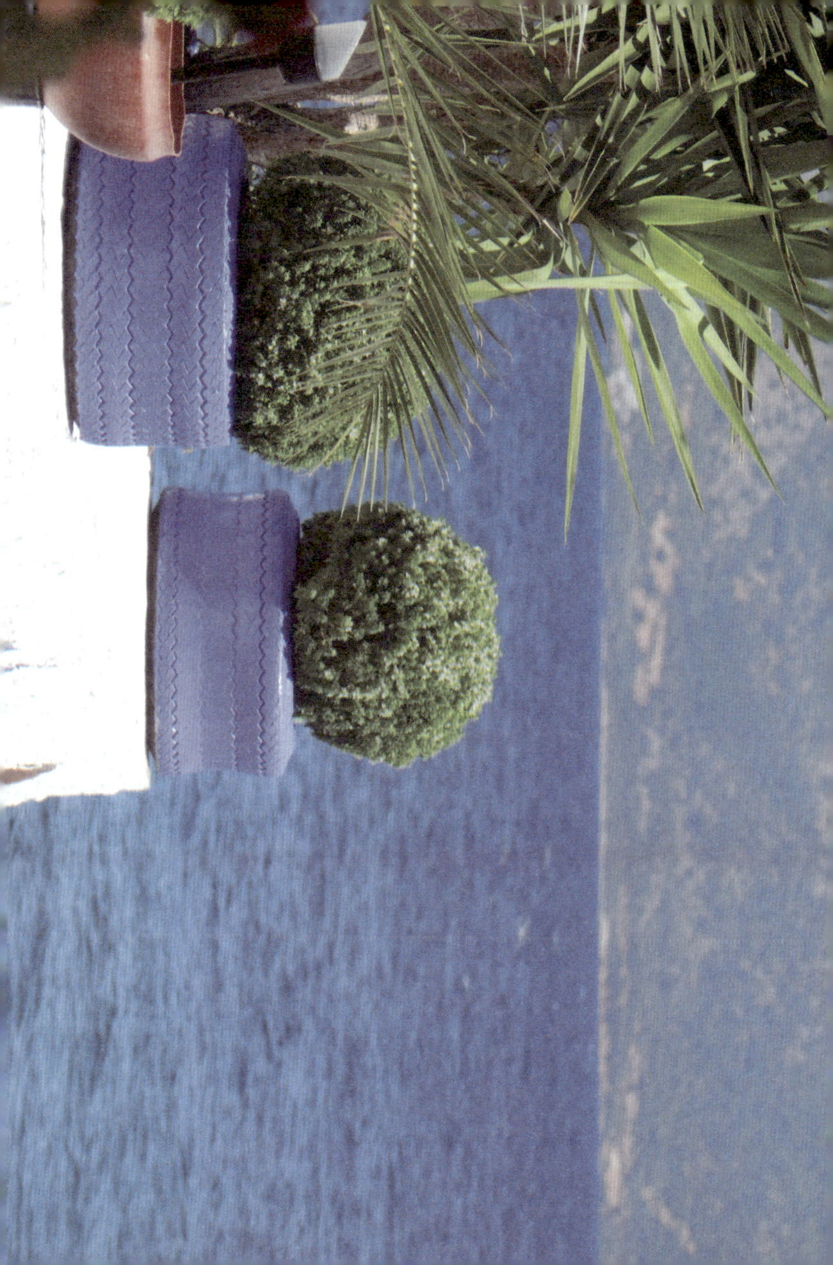

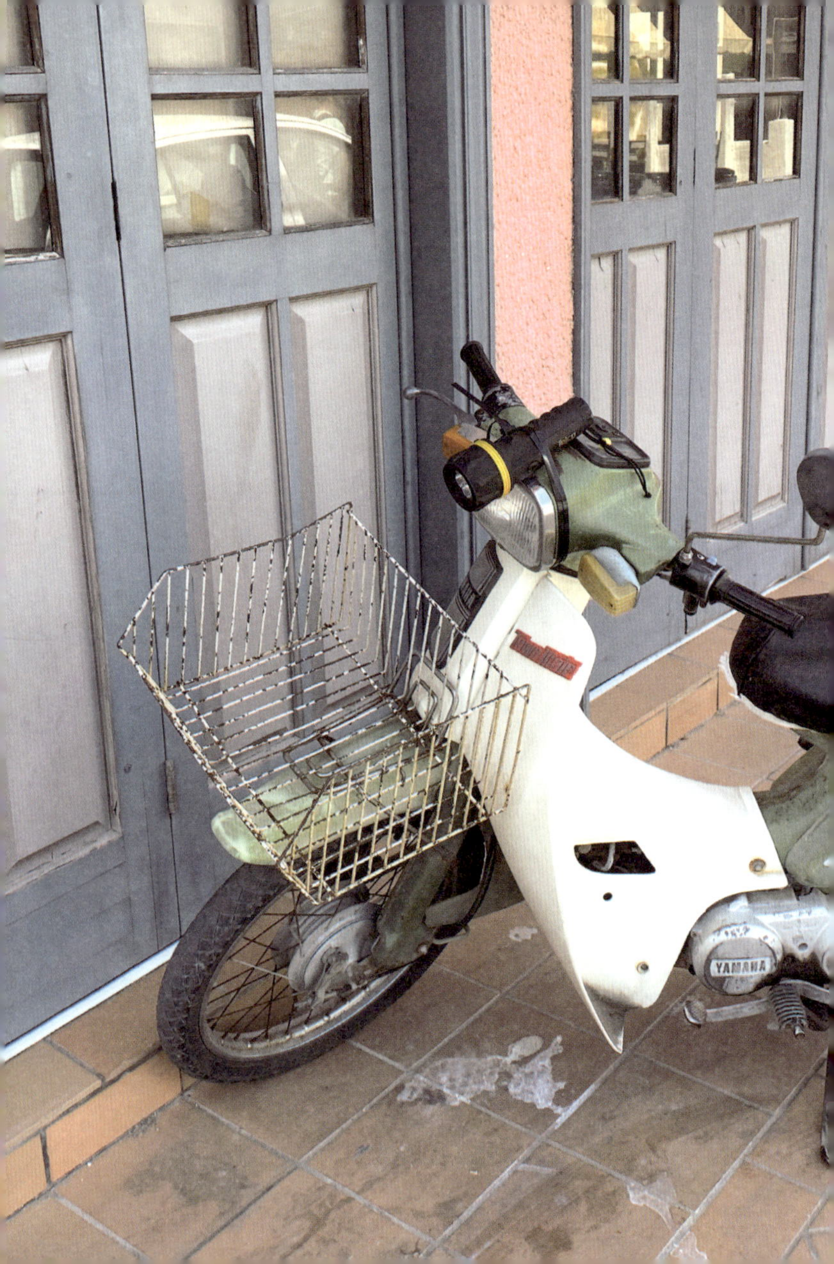
YAMAHA

Headlight

Tie wraps, tape, hand-torch

Aegina

Papairlines

Buoy
Plastic containers for ketchup & mayo, rope

Syros
Sotiris Patronis

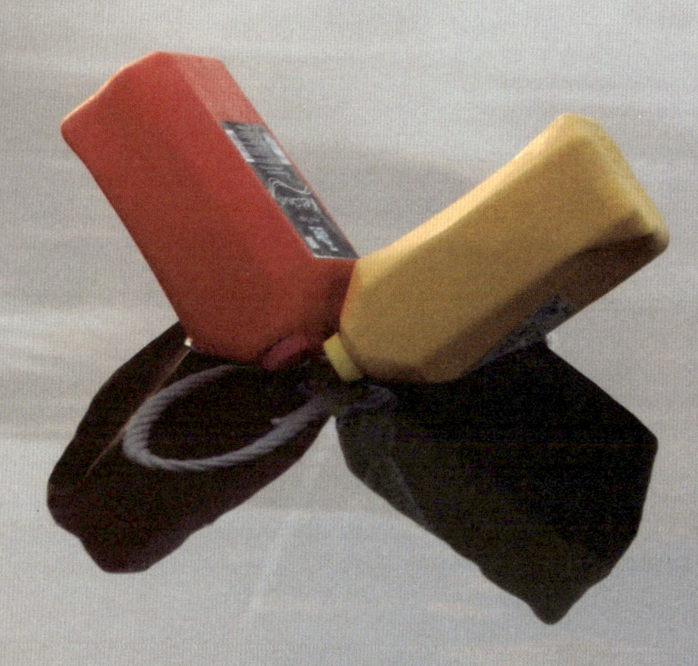

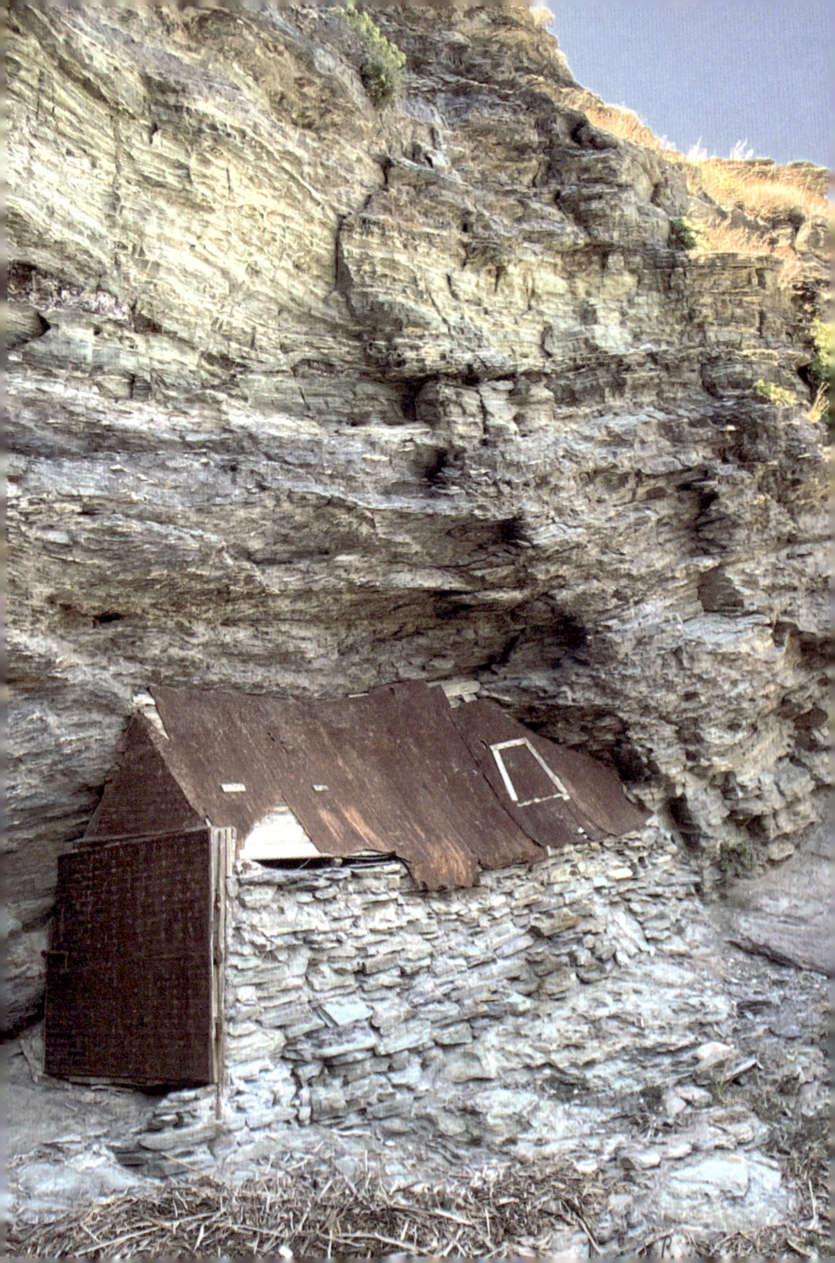

Beach hut

Reclaimed wood & other materials, stone

Pelion

Papairlines

Traffic cone tripod
Traffic cone, wooden slats, nails

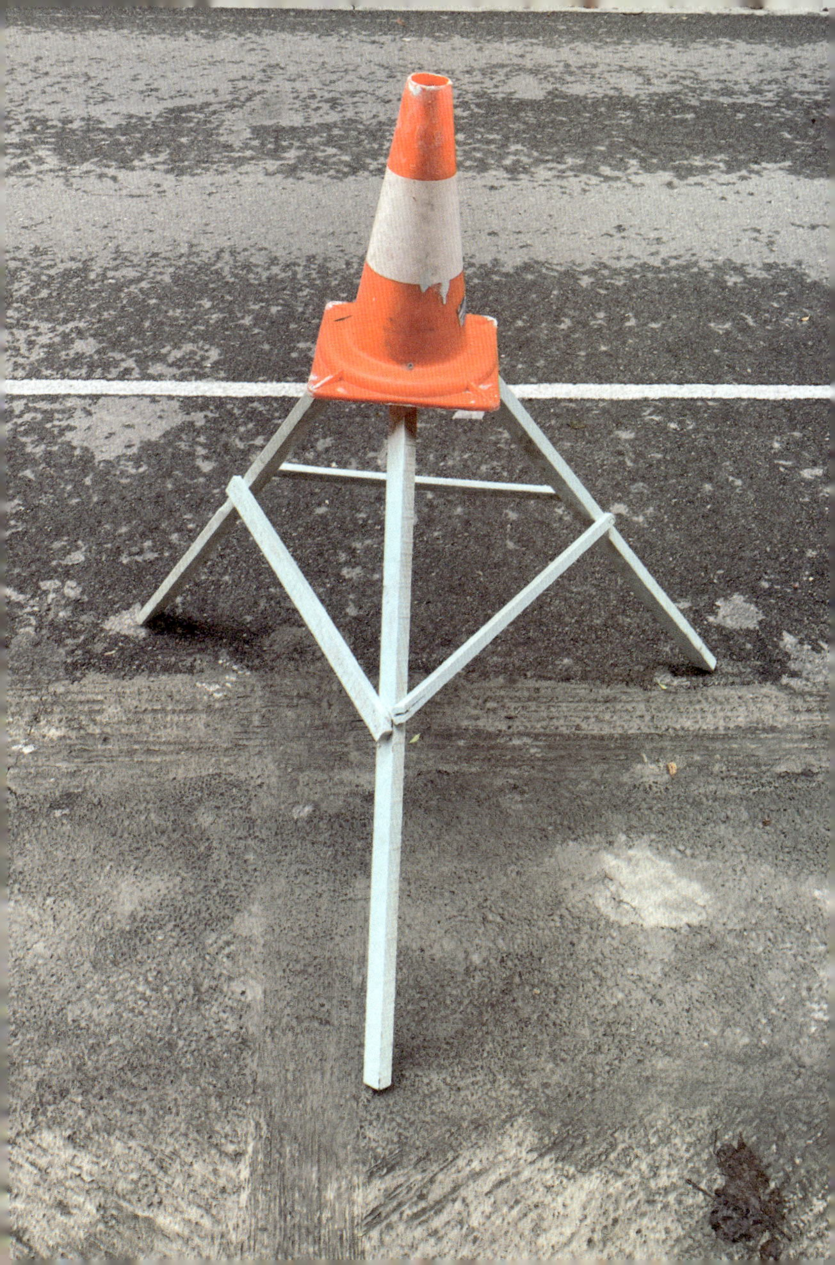

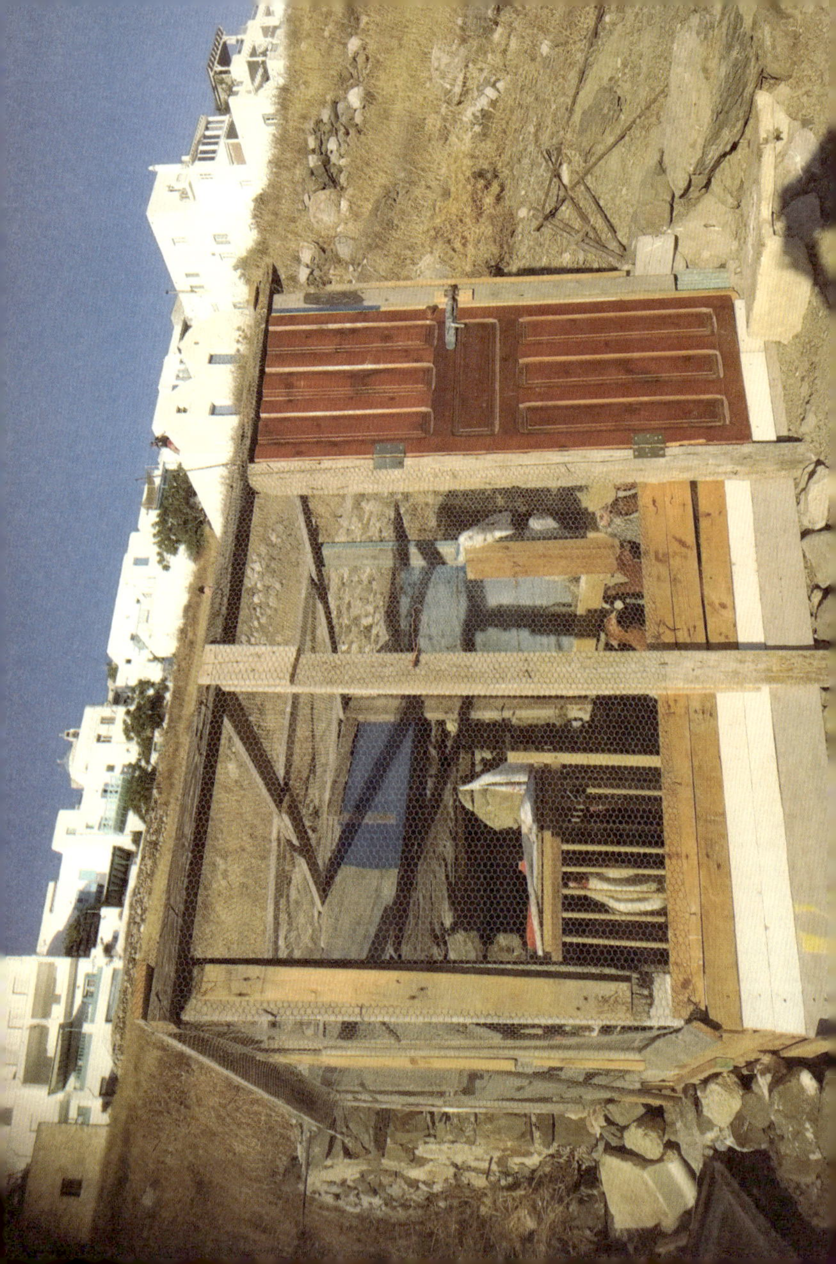

Chicken coop
Reclaimed wood, vintage door, hinges, chickenwire

Astypalaia
Katerina Papastergiopoulou

Wall clock

Wooden flask, copper tray, clock mechanism, handmade clock hands, glass, marker

Athens

Maria Giannadaki

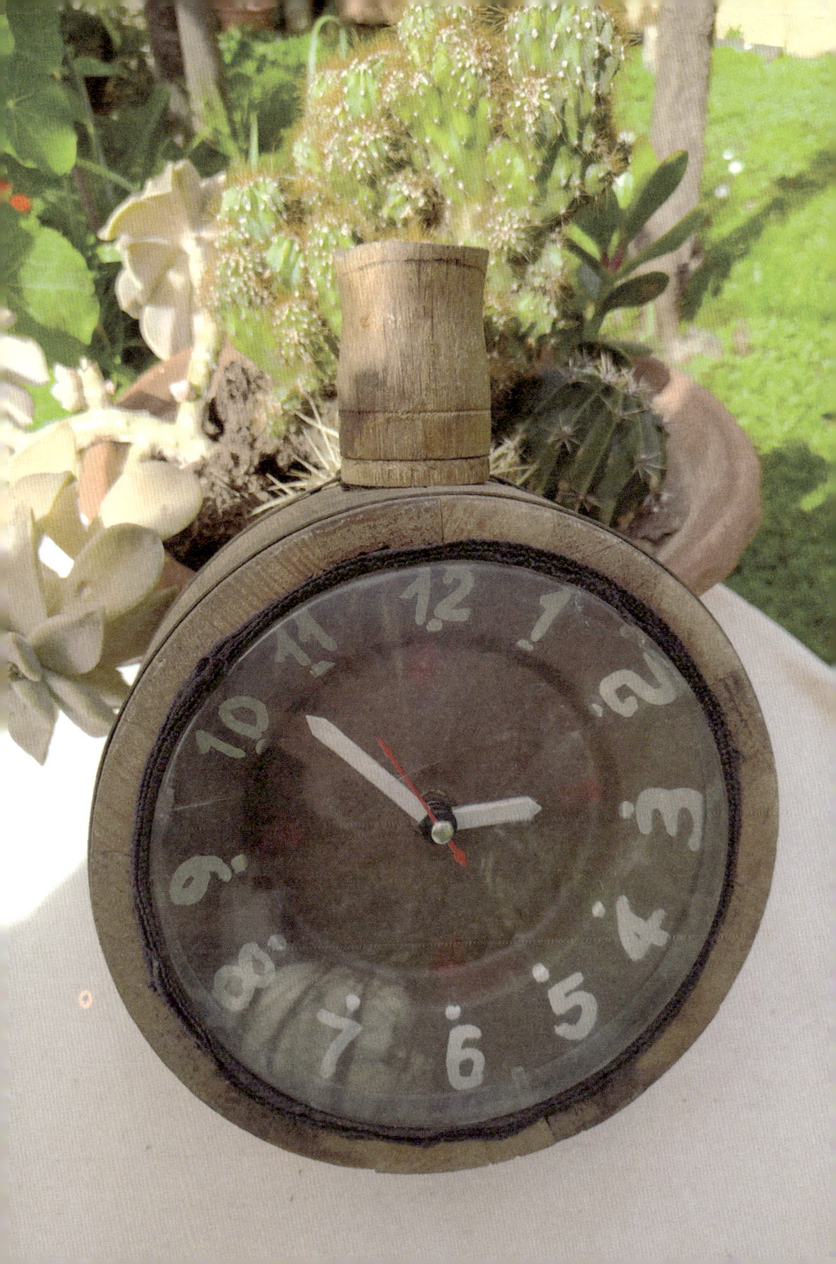

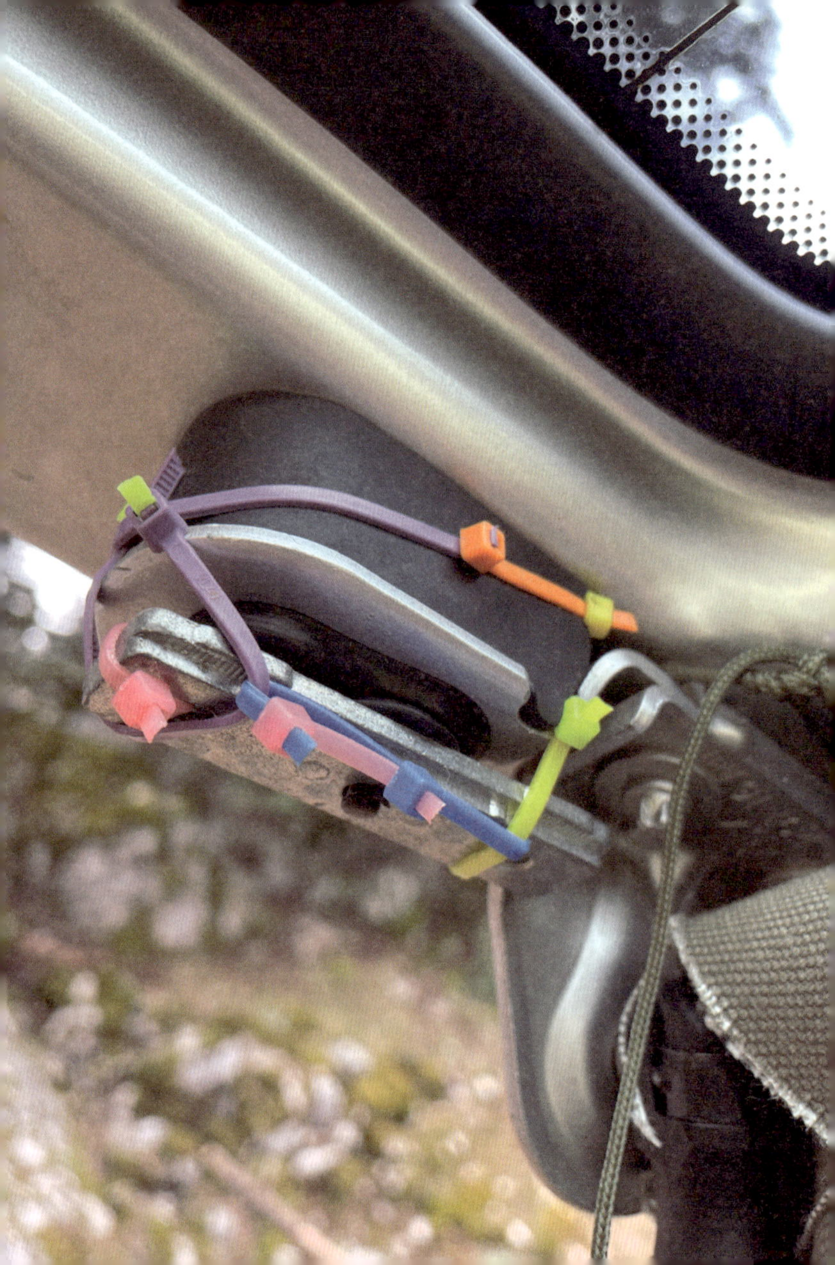

Perpetually off light switch

Tie wraps, metal plate

Having modified their vehicle with various contraptions to allow a person to sleep comfortably with the hatch open, here the designer has tie-wrapped a metal plate on the analog switch to keep the car boot light shut during the night. It saves the vehicle's battery.

Arachova
Papairlines

Patio decorations
Paint, dried pumkins

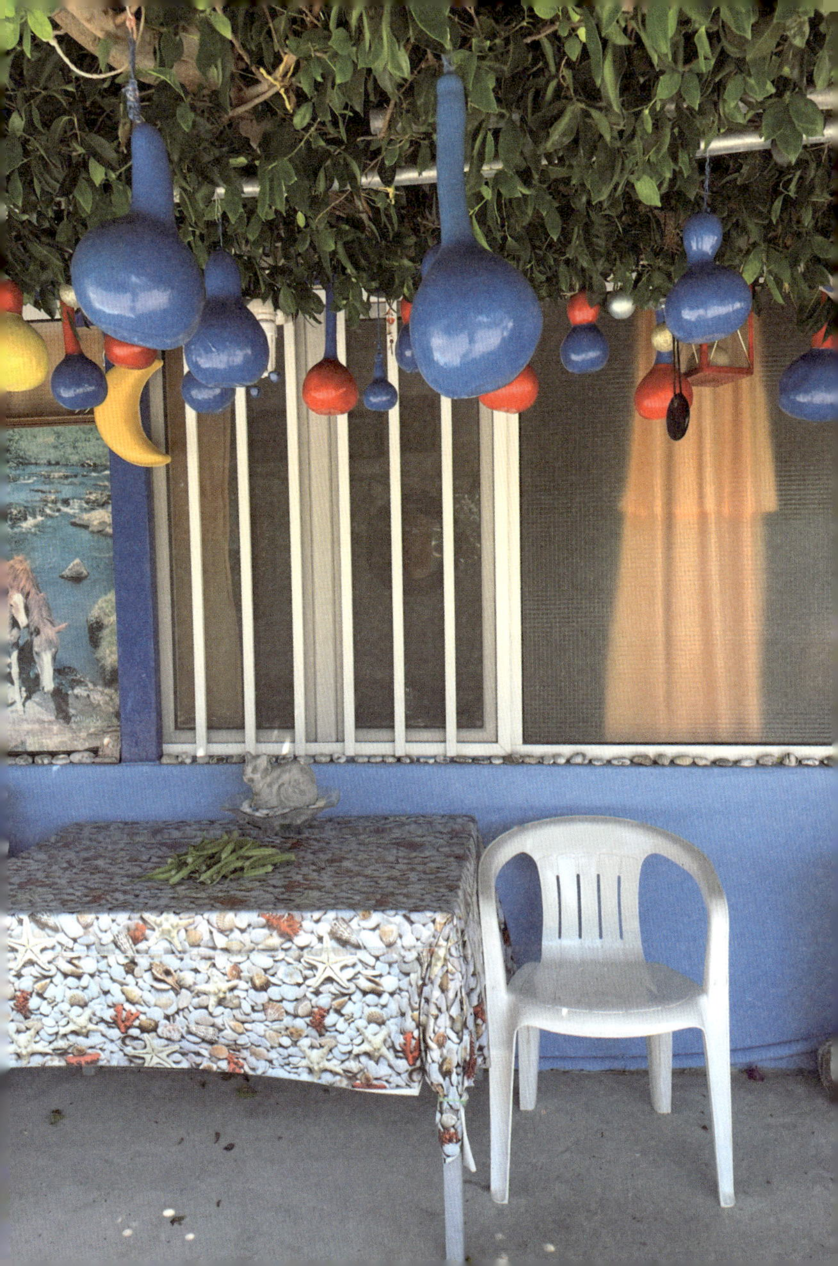

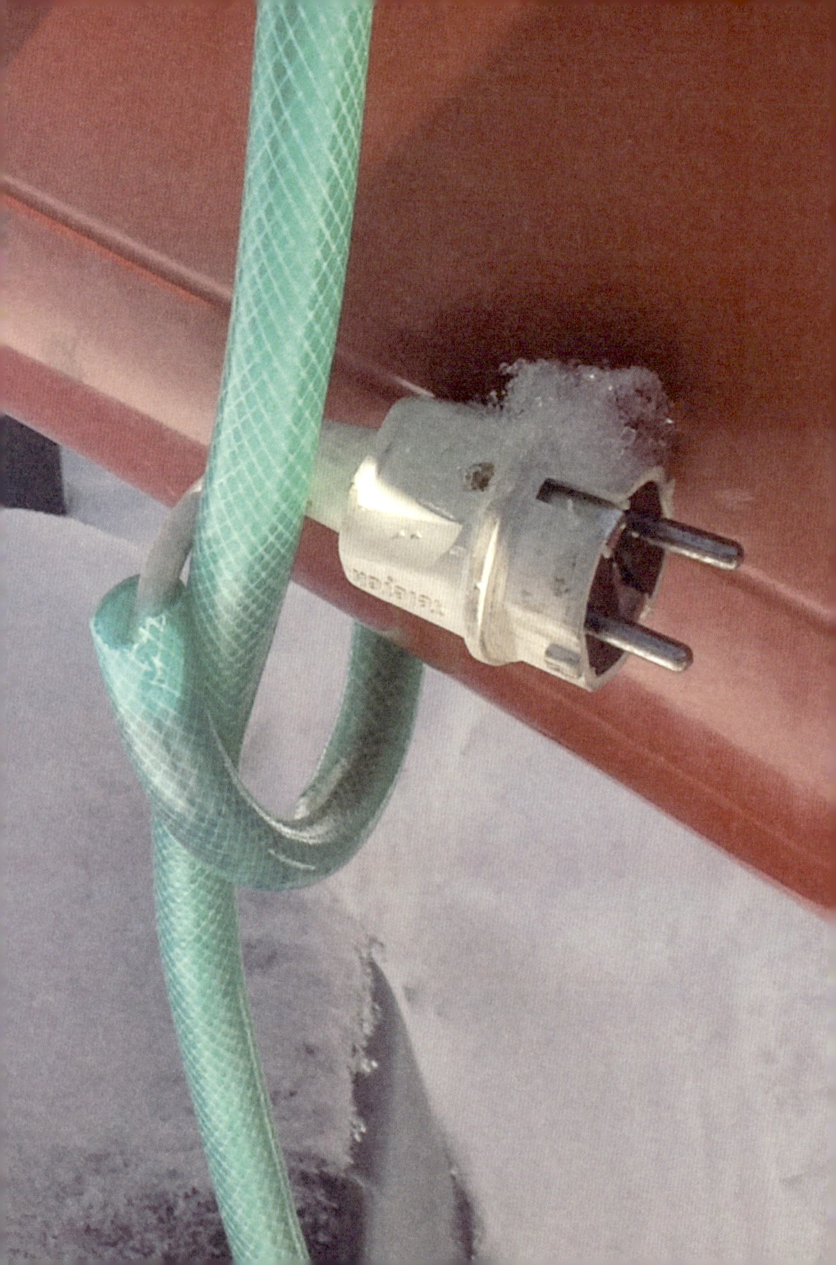

Cable waterproofing
Water hose, cable

Metsovo
Papairlines

Pavement railing
Yellow paint, net, branches, broom stick, string

Limited car parking spaces in Athens can make frustrated drivers act without much thought of their neighbors. A home entrance on the edge of the pavement is frequently used as a parking spot. In this case, the designer has created a DIY fence and painted the pavement to notify that this is not a parking spot. Now they can enter their home unobstructed.

Athens
Papairlines

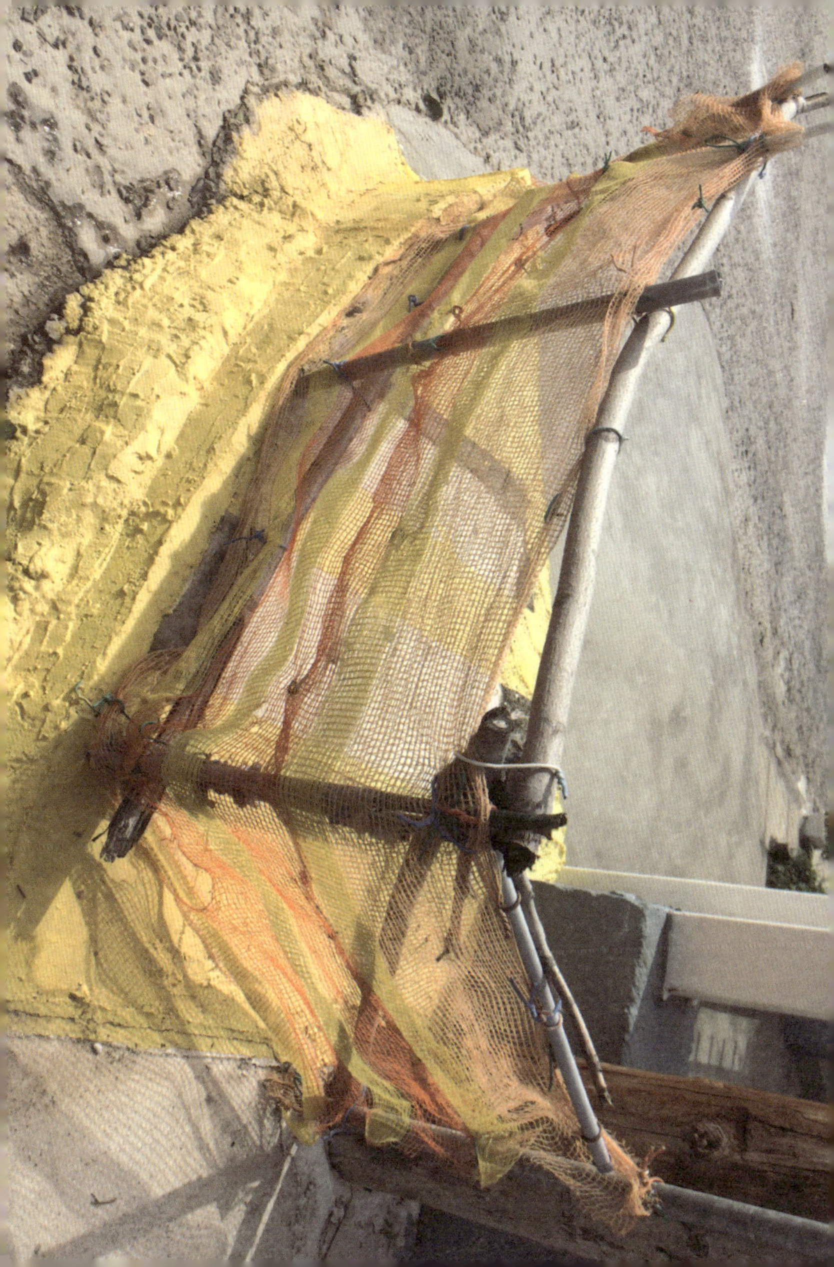

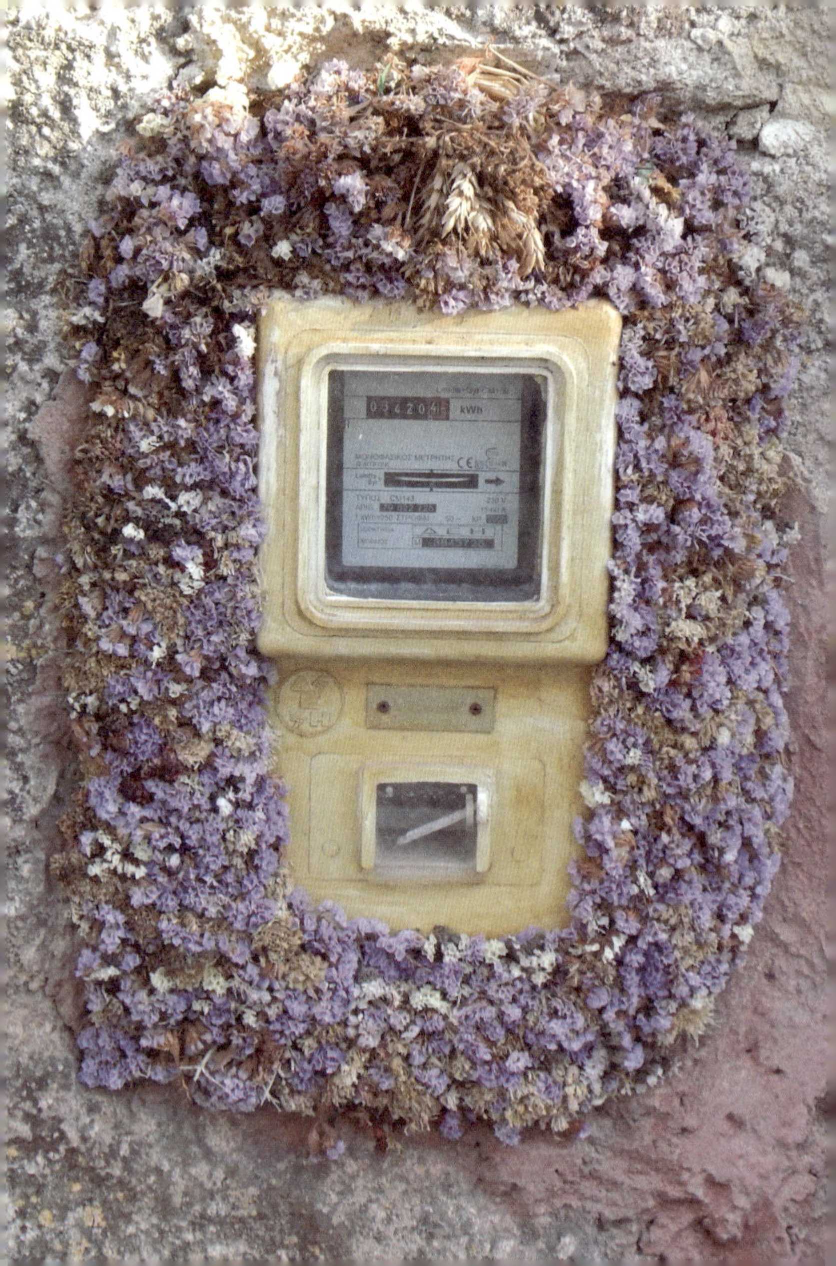
kWh
ΜΟΝΟΦΑΣΙΚΟΣ ΜΕΤΡΗΤΗΣ
CM143
230 V

Electricity meter decoration
Statice flowers, rope

Mitikas
Sotiris Patronis

Divider, beach shelter
Wooden pallets, timber beams

Mykonos
Sotiris Patronis

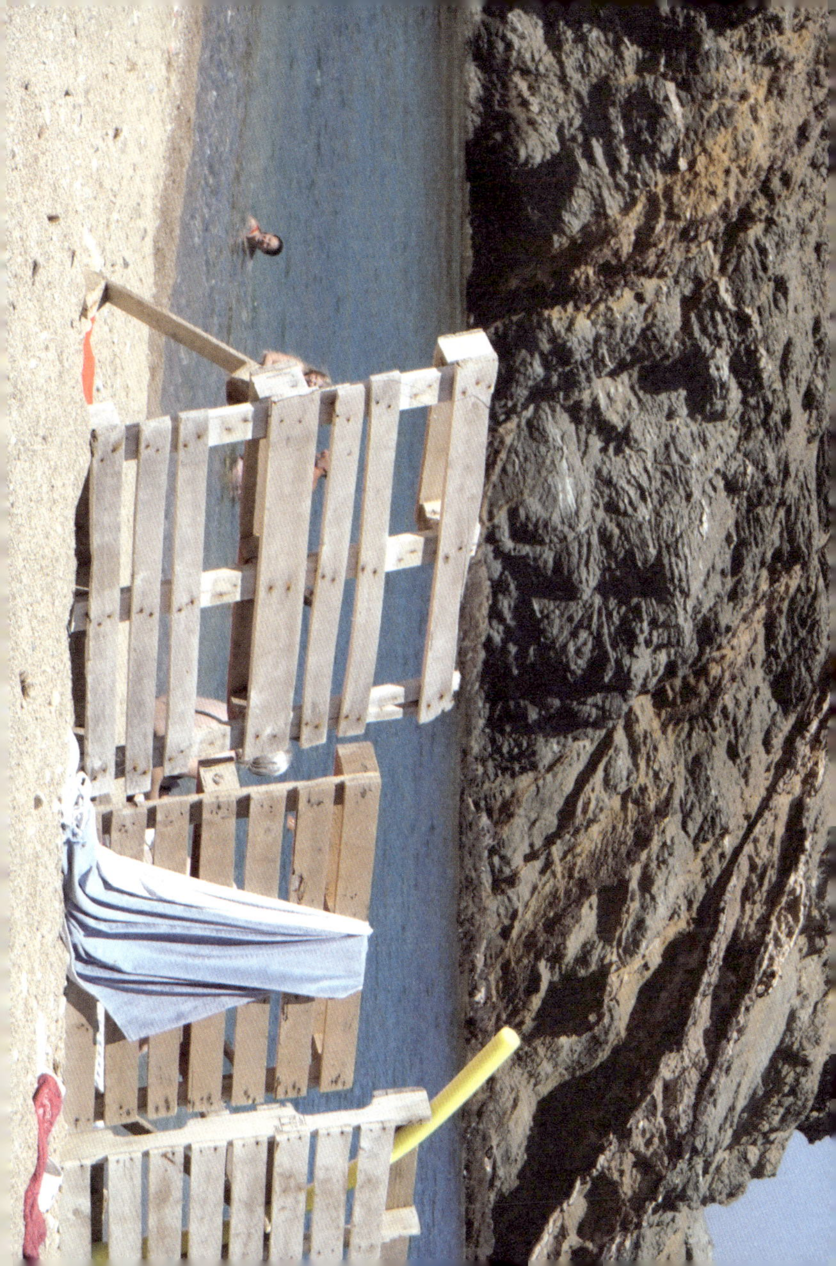

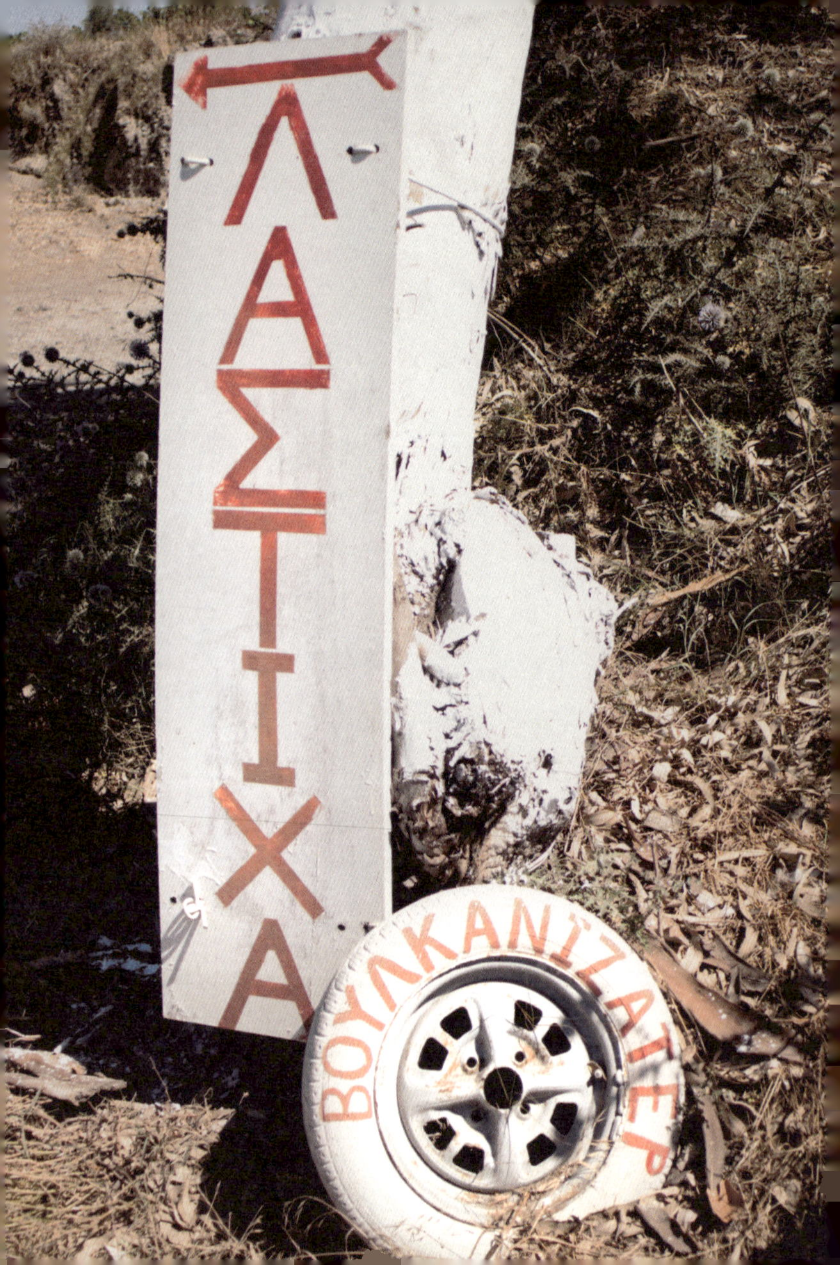
ΛΑΣΤΙΧΑ
ΒΟΥΛΚΑΝΪΖΑΤΕΡ

Outdoor signboard
Paint, tire, MDF

Santorini
Michalis Vlavianos

Rubbish basket
Reclaimed wood

Amorgos
Sotiris Patronis

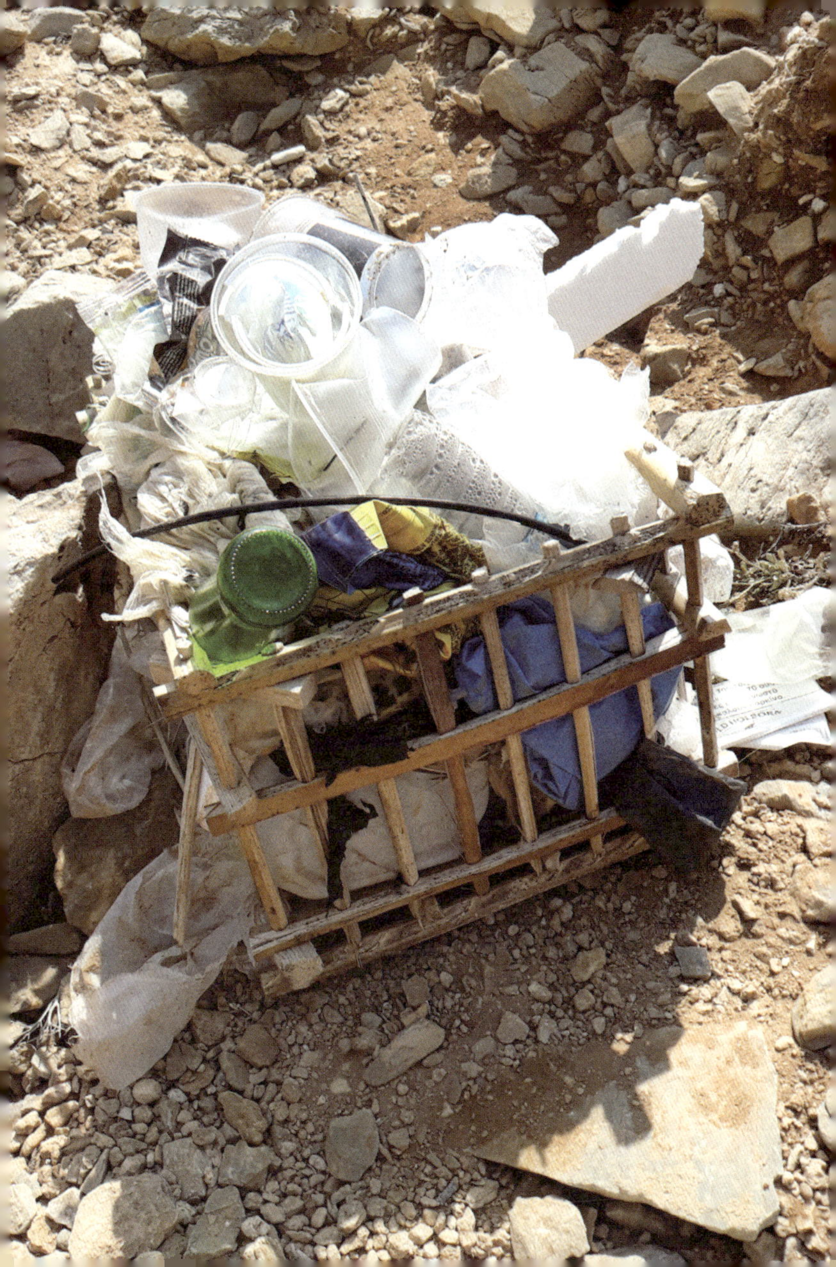

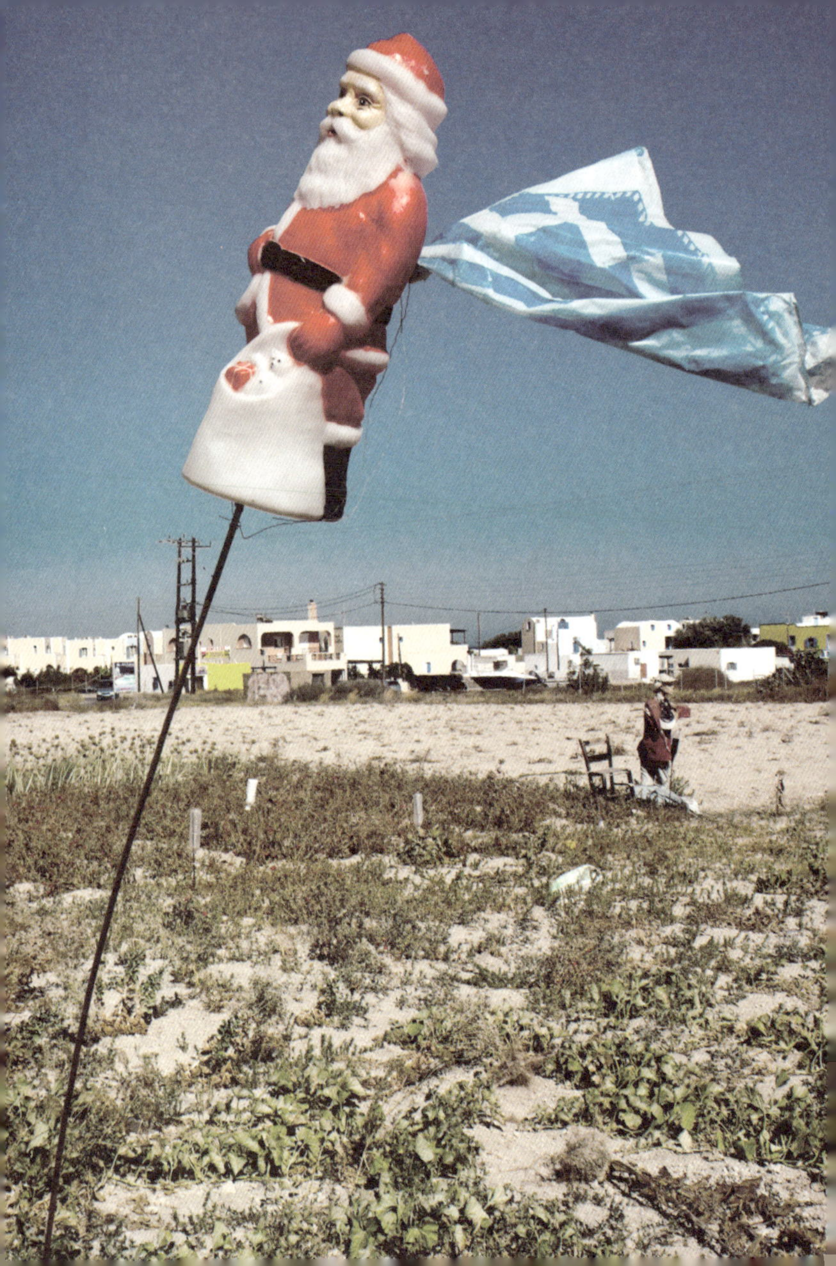

Scarecrow
Plastic Santa, plastic flag, metal rod

Santorini
Papairlines

Glass brick fence

Glass bottles, cement

Lefkada

Sotiris Patronis

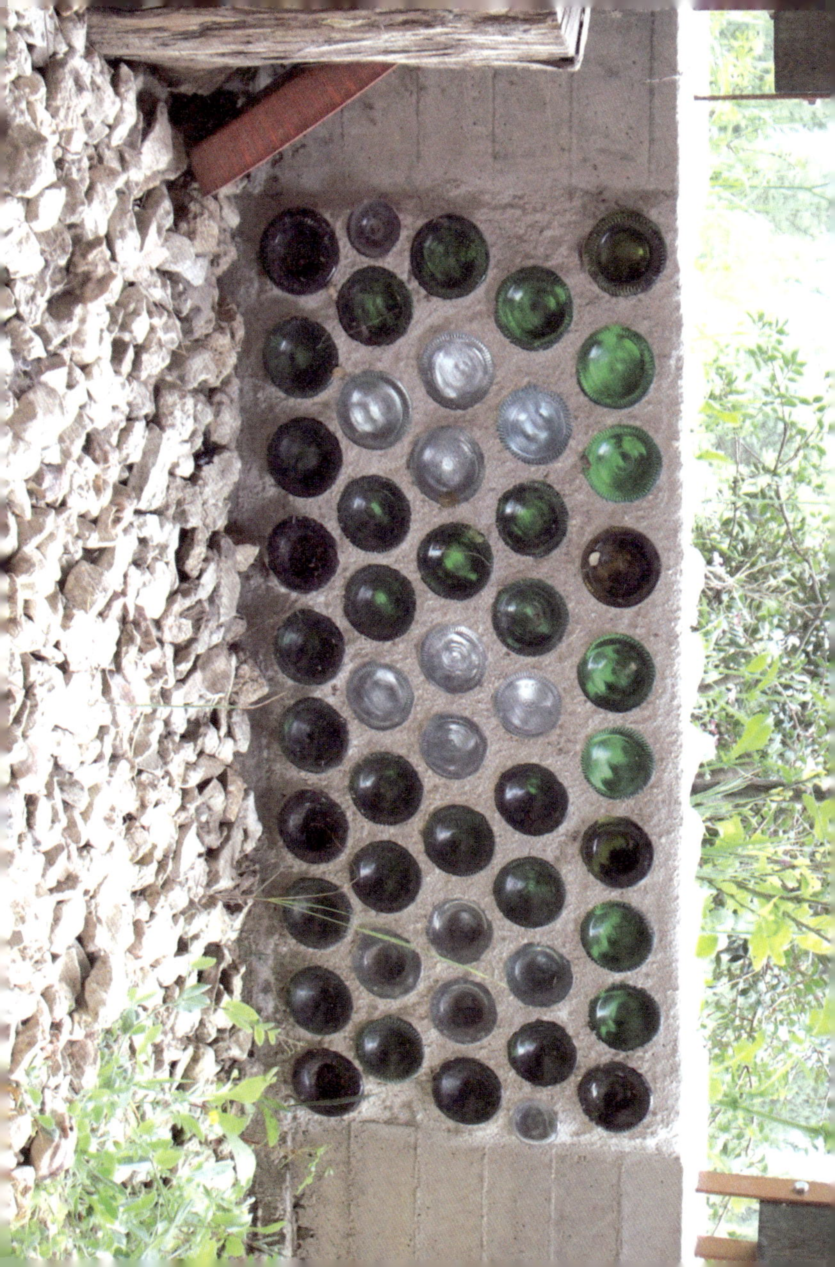

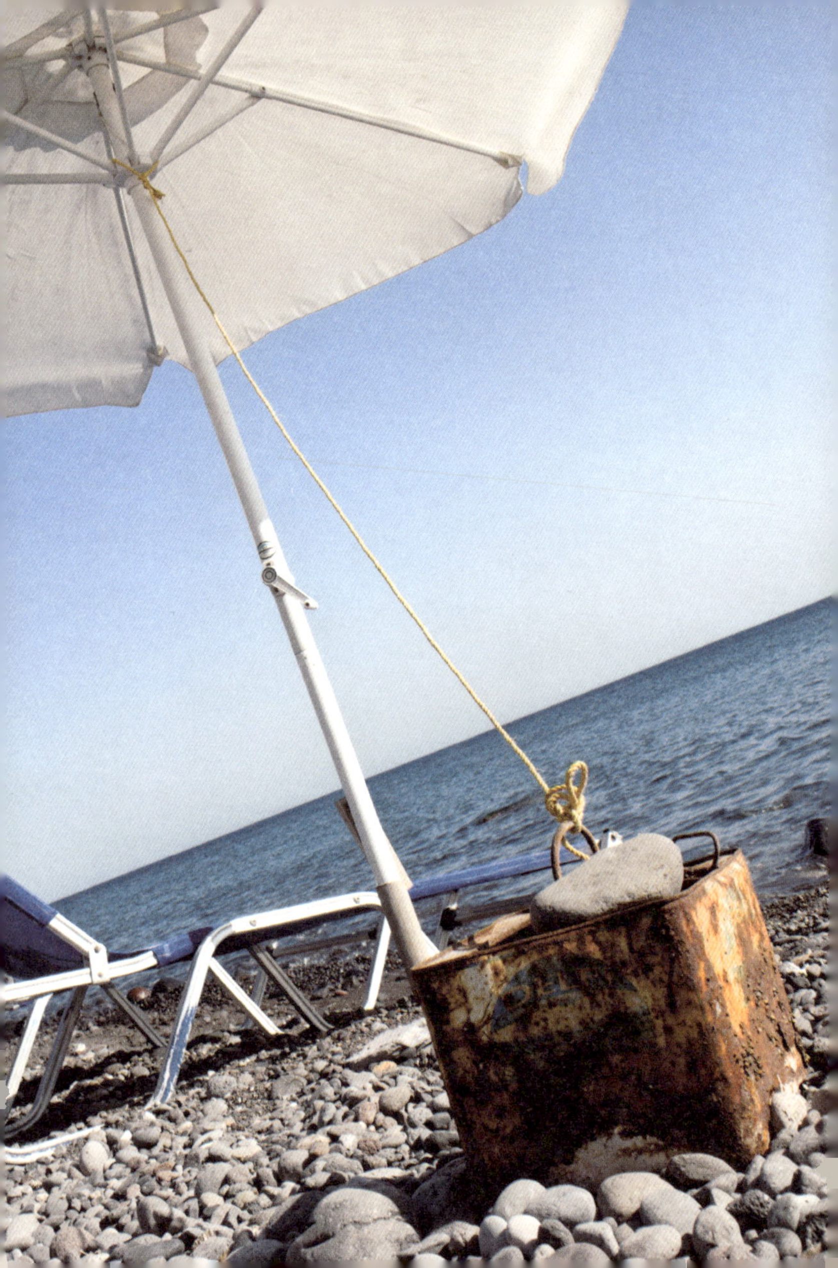

Beach umbrella base

Feta cheese tin container, concrete, stone, rope

Surveilance system
Discarded car mirrors

The window being at street level requires some precautions to be taken. Whether to protect any passersby from a sudden opening of the window, or to be used as a surveillance device, protecting the housekeeper from unwanted visitors. However, it seems that these mirrors cover both needs.

Chania
Gosia Cyganowska

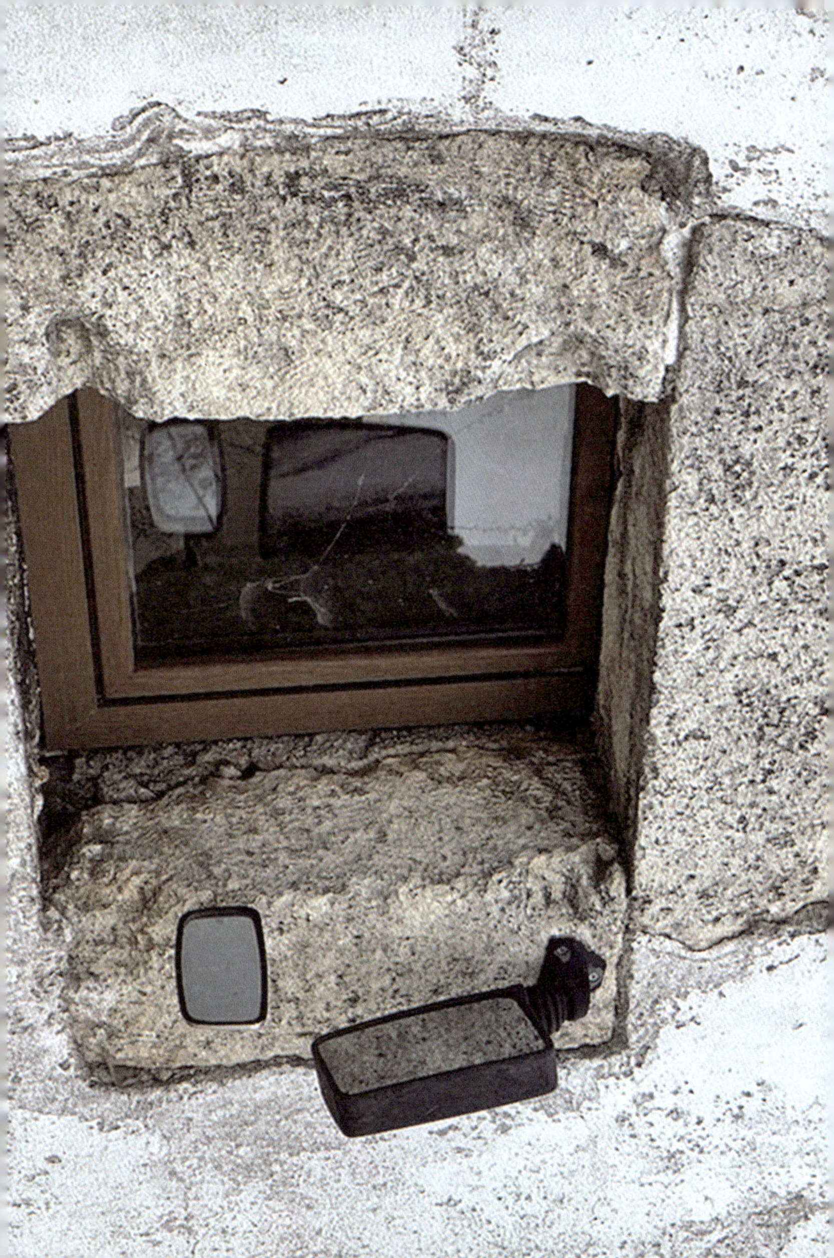

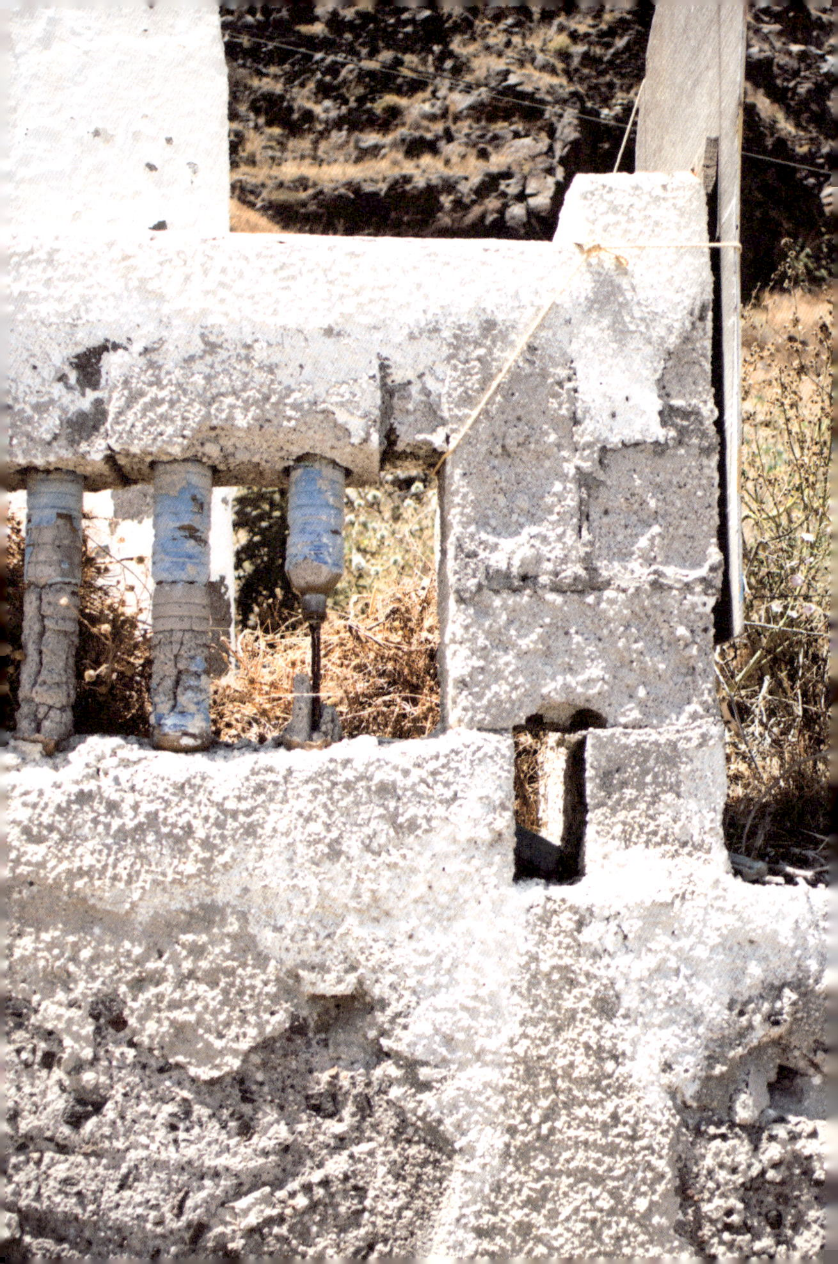

Railing

Cement blocks, rods, plastic water bottles, concrete, plaster

Santorini
Michalis Vlavianos

Bumper
Tree trunk

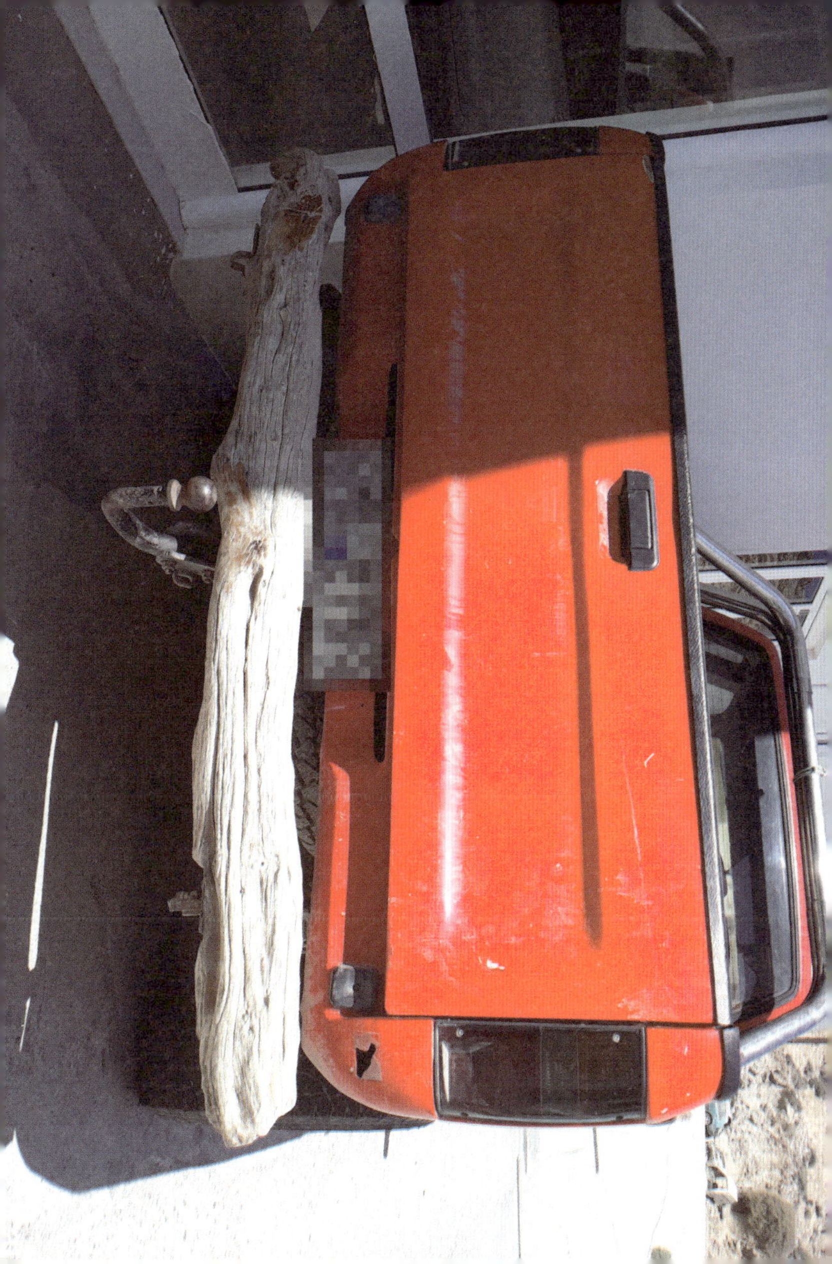

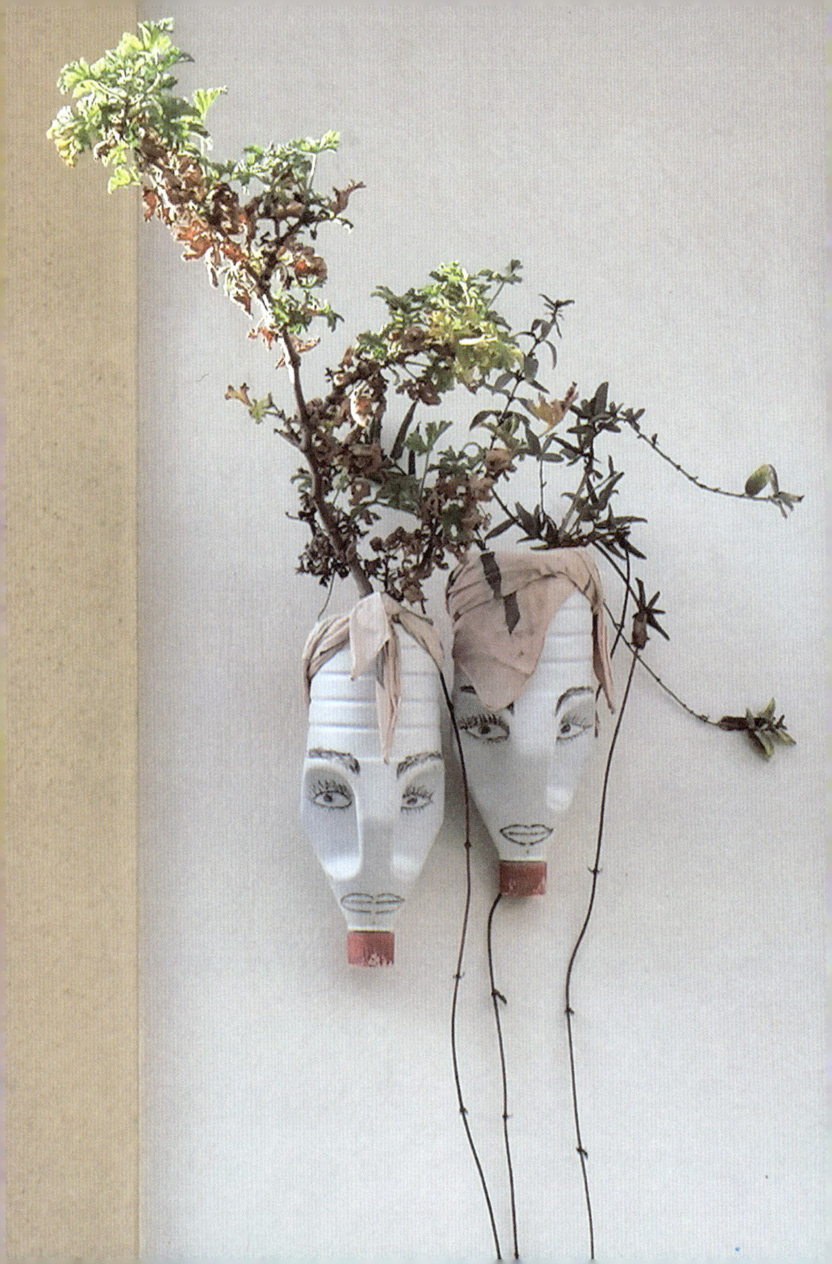

Planters
Plastic containers, white paint, black marker, fabric

Chiliomodi
Spyros Drakos

Barbeque
Half a water heater, metal frame, metal joist, car wheel

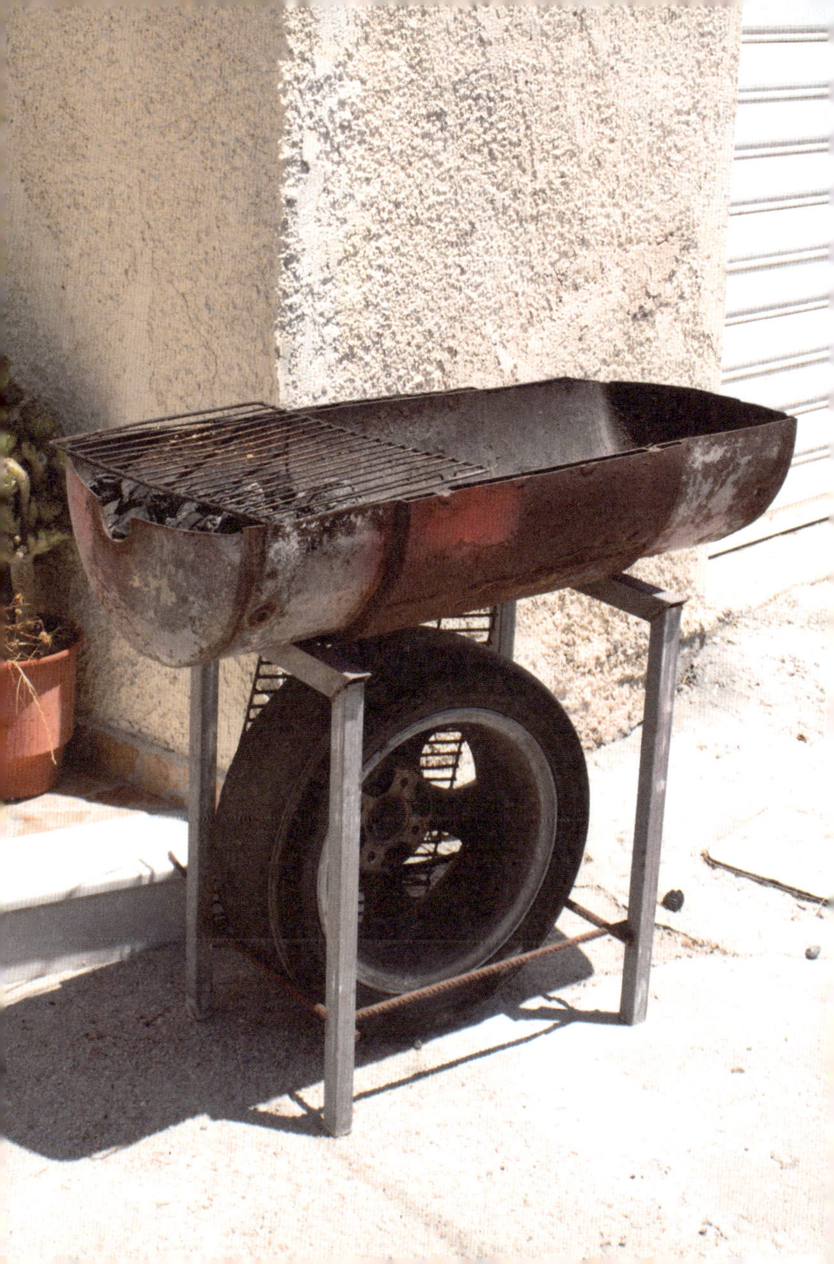

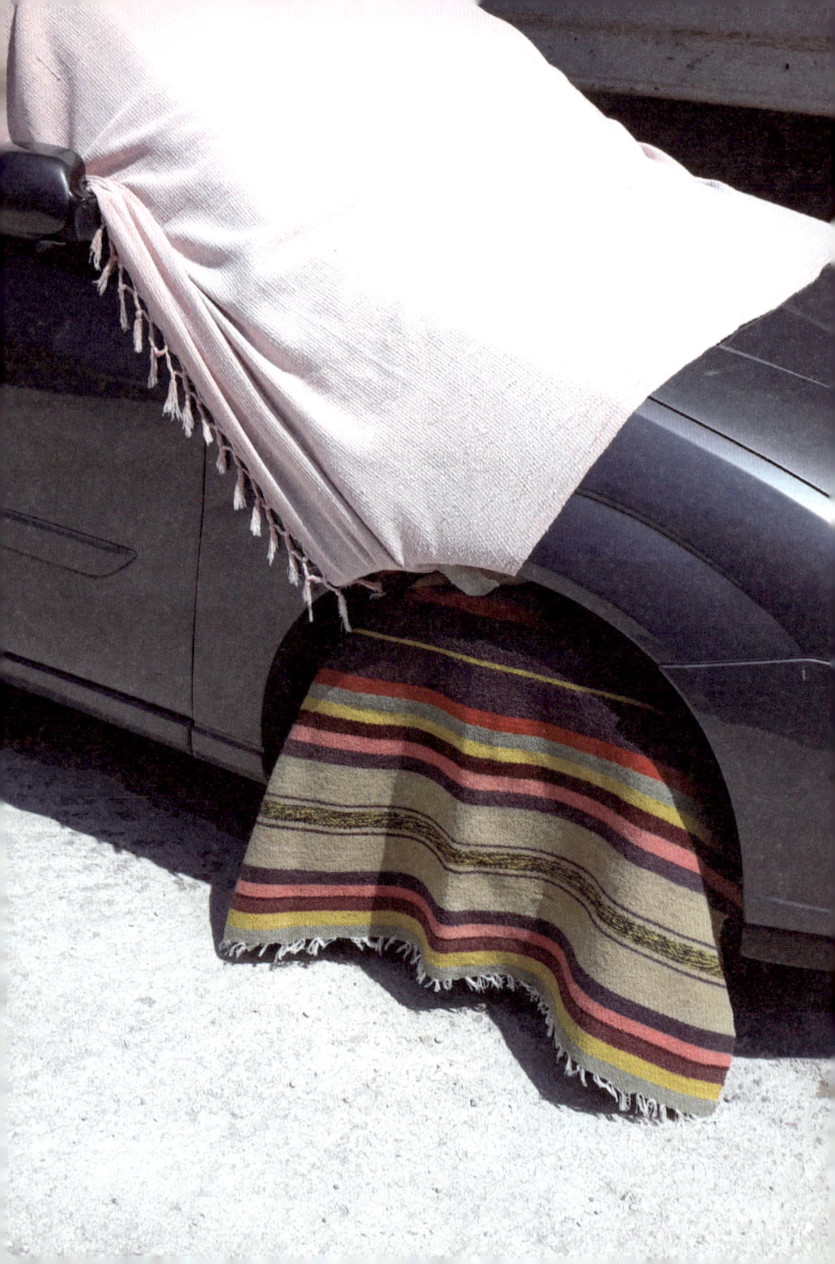

Sun protection cover
Kilim, cotton blanket

Mesolongi
Sotiris Patronis

Outboard motor
Drill, propeller

Naxos
Sotiris Patronis

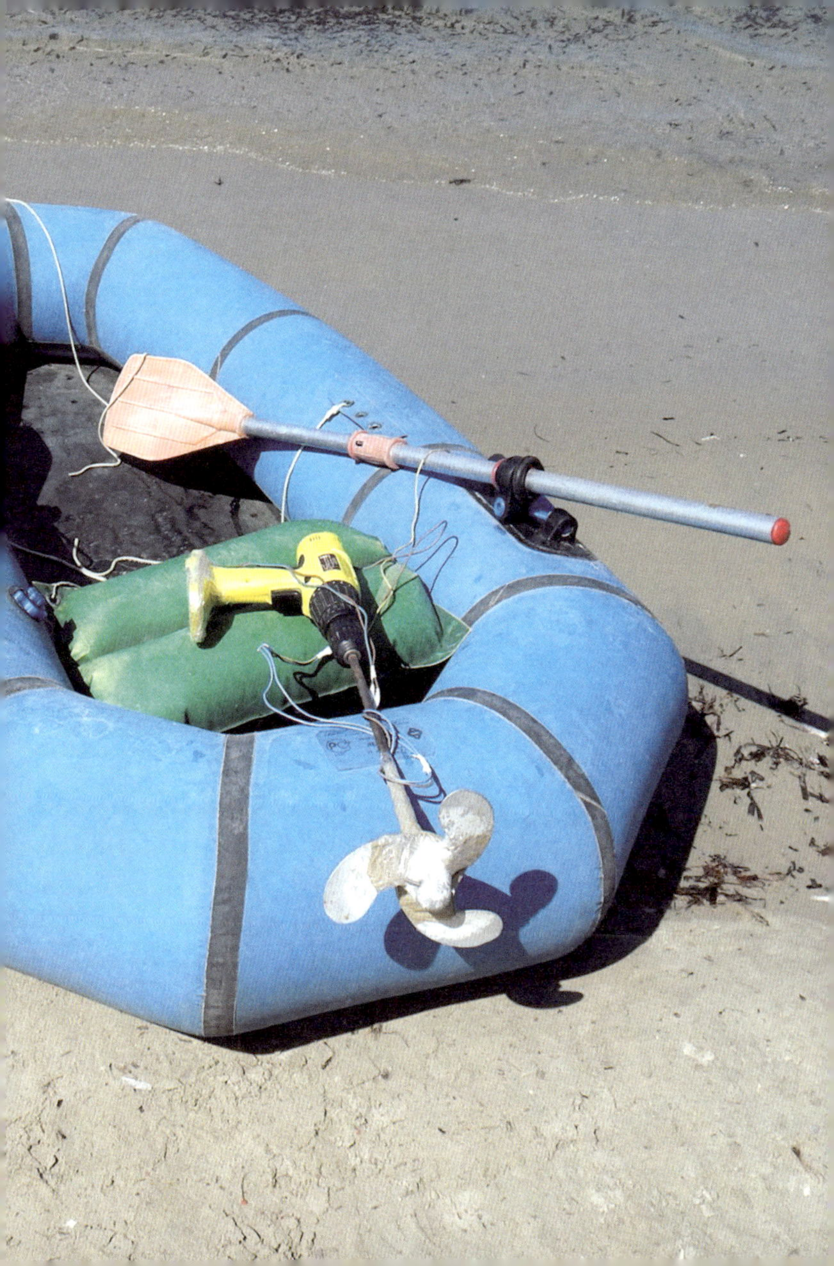

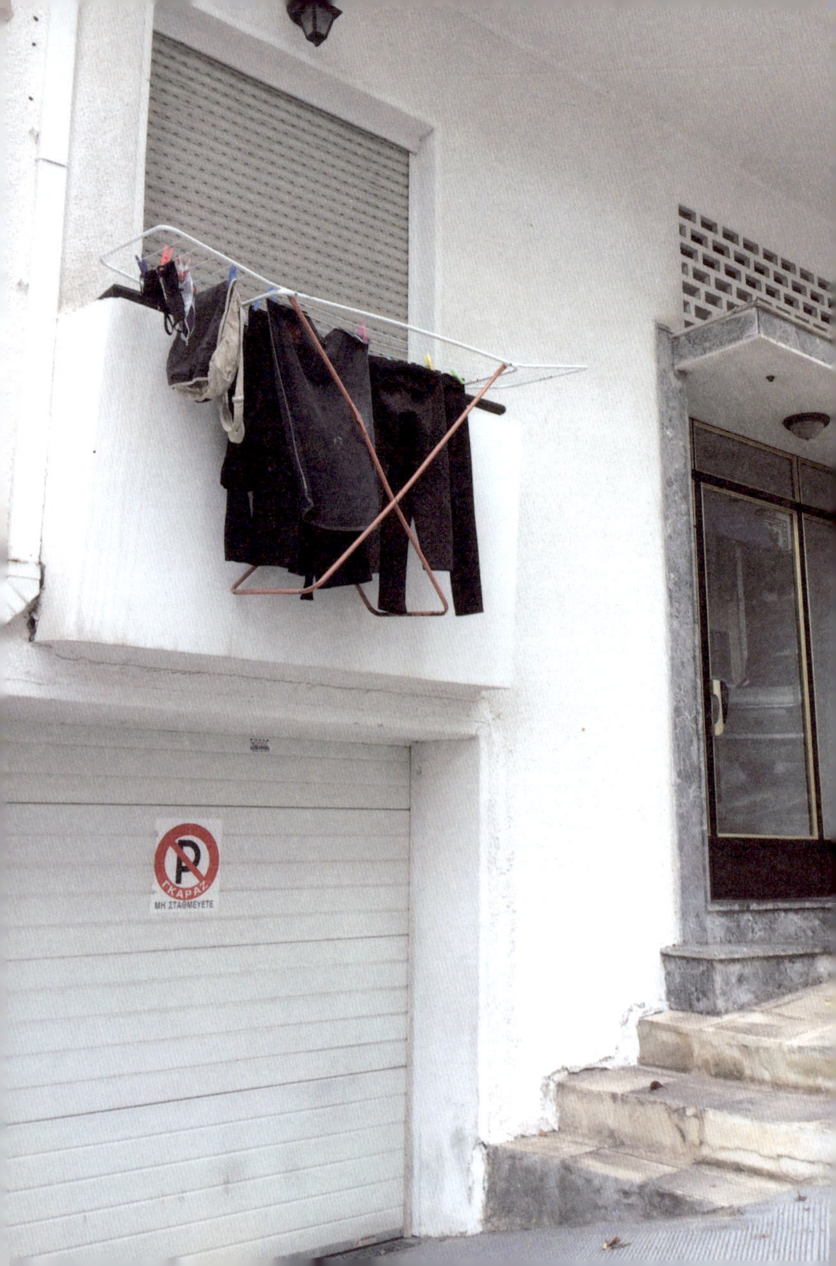
ΓΚΑΡΑΖ
ΜΗ ΣΤΑΘΜΕΥΕΤΕ

Freestanding drying rack, metal wire

Quite a few blocks of flats built in Athens feature small apartments. Most, due to building regulations, have non-existent balconies, so drying laundry can be challenging. This DIY designer has extended their apartment space outside their flat.

Stage for the band
Plastic crates, MDF sheets

In local folk festivals a.k.a. "panigyris", around the country, the orchestra is raised from the dancefloor to see and be seen. Here, the DIY designer uses bright coloured retsina wine crates to achieve this function. An action inspiring a promising celebration!

Metsovo
Papairlines

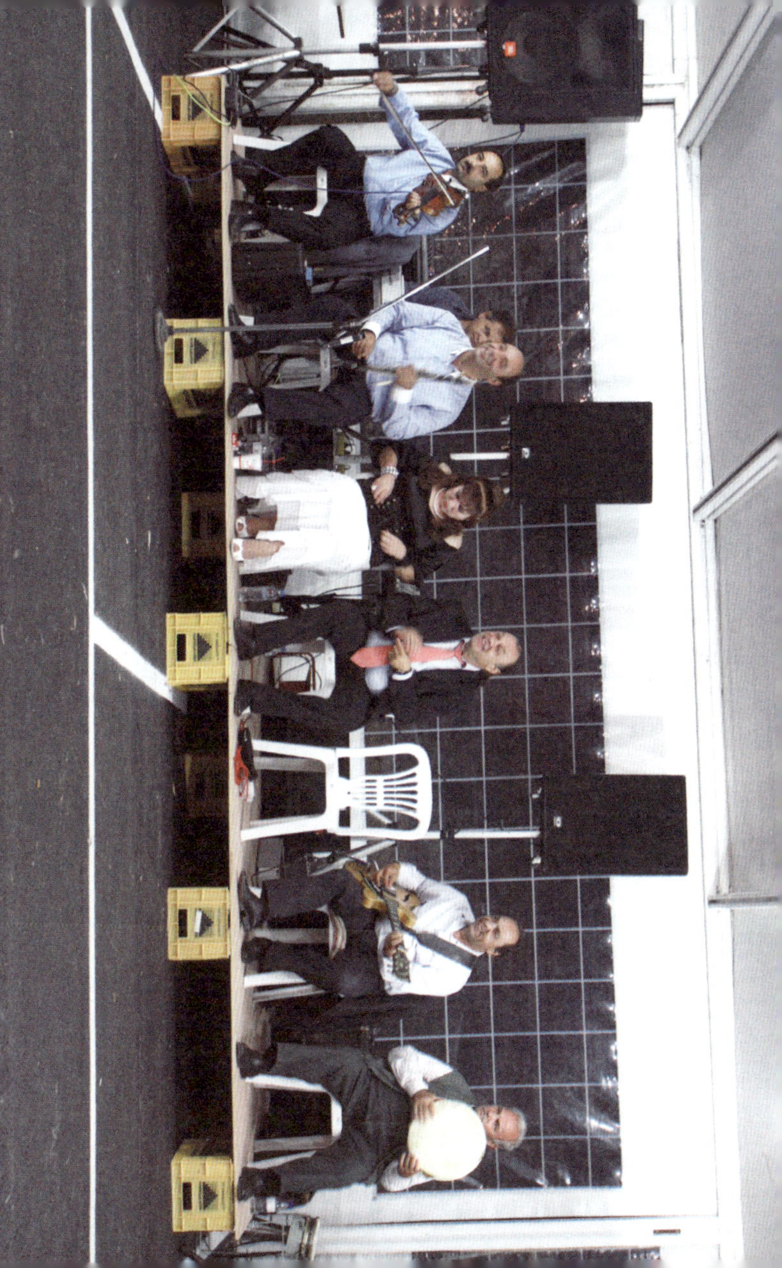

We would like to thank all the participating photographers, the Department of Product and Systems Design Engineering of the University of the Aegean, Damianos Gavalas and Irini Rigopoulou, the Research Lab for Computational Design and Digital Fabrication of the Department of Product and Systems Design Engineering of the University of Western Macedonia, Panagiotis Kyratsis, Athanasios Manavis, Nikolaos Efkolidis and their students, Nikos Predoulis for looking after the copyright, Sebastian Collins for the initial proof reading, Andreas Kokkino for the final copy editing, Dimitris Fakinos for spreading the word, Åsa Ståhl for her thoughts and insights, Stathis Mitropoulos and Nina Gry Myschetzky for graphically adopting this project, and of course everyone that responded to the open call but their photos did not make it to the pages of this book. Finally, we would like to thank all the creators of the ingenious objects in the photos and all the aspiring DIY creators out there!

Travelogue:
Greek everyday solutions to common problems
Curated by Loukas Angelou, Vasso Asfi, Costas Bissas

Designed by Stathis Mitropoulos
& Nina Gry Myschetzky

Copy editing by Andreas Kokkino

Printed by Pletsas-Kardari printing house
in an edition of 1000 copies

Published by Hyper Hypo

Athens, April 2024

This in an ongoing project and we are always on the lookout for new material, so if you have any images you would like to share, please send them to papairlines@gmail.com

www.papairlines.org

ISBN: 978-618-86646-4-7